# An Unfamiliar Path...
### how cancer led us deeper into the heart of God

*"I will lead the blind by ways they have not known, along unfamiliar paths I will guide them; I will turn the darkness into light before them and make the rough places smooth. These are the things I will do; I will not forsake them."*
Isaiah 42:16

# Lori U. Hearn
## Forewords by
### Mike Hearn , Davis Hearn, & Mallory Hearn

Revised Edition 2019

ISBN: 9781071111635

I hope you enjoy this book, and I pray that God will somehow use it to encourage you as you journey through a crisis or as you journey alongside someone going through a crisis. In our humanness, it is normal to struggle in our faith and trust in God. He knows our weaknesses, yet He has made a way for us to rest in His love and care when our world is shaken and turned upside down by trials and troubles. Jesus is our Rock and our Redeemer, and if we allow Him to, He will walk with us every step of the way as we journey through life...especially along unfamiliar paths!

Published by
Lori Hearn

# ~Contents~

# ~Dedication~

THIS BOOK IS DEDICATED to my amazing husband, Mike! I love you more than words can express and you have taught me the true meaning of living life with purpose...without ever saying a word! Your courage, perseverance, faith, and trust in God are a true testimony to the power and peace available to those who place their hope in our sovereign, faithful Lord – Jesus Christ. Thank you for holding my hand on this journey when I should have been holding you up and for living a "more than victorious" life as a result of what Jesus has done in and for you! You are my hero and my knight in shining armor!

# ~Acknowledgments~

WHERE DO I BEGIN?  Without the love and support of our family, friends, and church, we would have never survived this journey – physically, emotionally, and spiritually.

To both sets of our parents we say, "Thank you!" Your constant support and encouragement have sustained us and rescued us on many occasions.  Without your constant love and care, this journey would have had far more bumps and dead ends along the way.  I hope our appreciation has been evident and without question.

To our children...there are truly no words to accurately express how incredibly proud we are of you and just how amazed we are by your faith and perseverance.  We can only hope and pray that God will use this time in your life to inspire you and equip you to take up your cross and follow Christ in every area of your life.  God has amazing plans for each and every stage of your life.  We have never doubted that!  We trust completely that God will use every challenge and trial we have faced for your good and for His glory to be manifested in and through your lives.  We love you both and our greatest privilege is to have been given the responsibility of being your parents!

I am not even going to begin to thank the individuals who have come alongside us throughout this journey.  It would be impossible and too lengthy to mention them all by name (not to mention I would probably leave someone out!).  However, I will take this opportunity to sing the praises of each and every one of you.  You know who you are! We love you with every inch of our hearts.  To think of what this journey would have been like without you all is truly a nightmare! You have loved us, cared for us, fed us, prayed for us, encouraged us, made us laugh, held our hands when we cried, and walked with us each step of the way.  You are truly the picture of Christ, His love, His grace, and His faithfulness.  There has NEVER been a moment that we did not know, without a shadow of a doubt, that you were there to lift us up and carry us to the throne room. All we know to say is "Thank You" and "We love you with all our hearts."

I would also like to thank all those involved in Mike's medical care. You are angels sent from above! It is difficult to express just how much you have served as a buffer, protecting us from fear and dread. From Mike's neurosurgeon (Dr. Joshua Miller) to his local oncology team at Thompson Cancer Survival Center in Knoxville, TN, to the amazing team at the Preston Robert Tisch Brain Tumor Center at Duke University...you have all been a God-send! Thank you...thank you...thank you!

And finally, but most importantly, we say thank you to our gracious and faithful heavenly Father and our Savior, Jesus Christ. You, and You alone, deserve all the glory and honor and praise for all that we have received and been blessed by on this journey. If Your name has been lifted up by just one heart because of what we have been through, then every struggle...every heartache...every fear...every ounce of pain we have endured is worth it! We count everything as loss compared to how this journey has allowed us to see Your face and know You more intimately. We love you, Jesus, and we will NEVER stop singing Your praises! As long as we have breath...may our lives bring fame to Your name!

***"Let the name of the Lord be praised, both now and forevermore"***
Psalm 113:2

# ~Forewords~

## From Mike...

EVERYONE FACES DIFFICULTIES and challenges in life. These are often times that cause us to examine ourselves at a deeper level than normal. We are challenged to the very core of our beliefs when faced with a situation that could literally take our life away here on earth. When these situations arise, we quickly evaluate what is important and what is not. This book is about our family's journey over a period of about 15 months in the midst of one of these life-altering situations. On April 28, 2010 I was told I had a very serious mass in my brain that had the medical personnel scrambling to get me to a hospital that was equipped to meet my needs. My life will never be the same and that is the good news!

Early on in this journey, a special friend of ours sent us a passage of scripture to encourage us as we began to head down this dark, unfamiliar path. In fact, her mother had been traveling a very similar path for approximately a year and a half before my journey began. The scripture she shared was Isaiah 42:16 where God is speaking through His prophet, Isaiah, telling His people how He would faithfully lead them down unfamiliar paths and shine His light through the darkness so they could find their way. God promised to make the rough places smooth and not forsake them as long as they put their trust in Him. God has been faithful to fulfill this promise in our lives during this challenging and difficult journey into the unknown.

Our first reaction to the news was surprise and shock. When I went to the doctor that day in April, I had expected to be treated for a bad sinus infection. In reality, I was dealing with a much more serious issue. My wife and I knew this nightmare did not catch God by surprise, but it sure caught us off guard. Once the reality set in, we found ourselves clinging to the promises of God we had tucked into our hearts. We knew He would not leave or forsake us in our time of need. The diagnosis of stage IV brain cancer brought great uncertainty for me regarding my life here on earth, but I knew my eternal life was safe with Jesus.

God has taught us so much over the past year. We already knew the truths that God was reminding us of, but now He was displaying them to us like never before. We saw God answer prayers that no one else knew about and watched other people respond to God working in their lives to help and bless our family. One of the biggest blessings and yet hardest lessons we have learned has been trusting the truth that God uses adversity in our lives to deepen our relationship with Him. We can say we trust God, but when troubles come our way, the genuineness of our faith is tested by the fires of life. James 1: 2-4 says, "Consider it a great joy, my brothers, whenever you experience various trials, knowing that the testing of your faith produces endurance. But endurance must do its complete work, so that you may be mature and complete, lacking nothing." Trials are a necessity in the life of faith!

I would have never asked to have cancer. I would not have asked to be on this path that has the potential to be very scary. However, I would not trade what we have learned and the closeness to God that I have attained for anything. If I had to choose between having brain cancer and learning what we have learned over not having cancer yet missing out on what we have learned and the closeness to God that we have come to know, I would choose the path of cancer every time.

I am excited to share with you an opportunity to learn about our journey. I hope and pray that what you read in this book will encourage you or someone you know, or maybe our journey will enable you to reach out to and encourage someone going through a similar trial. I pray that God's grace, mercy, and hope will fill your heart. Most importantly, I pray that God's glory will be evident and that His name will be praised as a result of others reading our story.

# From Davis...

THE YEARS 2010 AND 2011 have been pretty crazy for my family. On April 28, 2010, my world was flipped totally upside down. When I found out that my dad had a golf ball size growth in his brain, I was shocked and scared of the unknown. While we were sitting in the hospital lobby on May 3 (the day my dad had surgery), the seriousness of our circumstances became more real. Although I was scared out of my mind, God was at work making sure we would be alright. The day Dad got home from the hospital, my mom got a job offer as a teacher at First Baptist Academy in Powell, TN. That was a huge blessing for our family and a great example of the many ways God provided for our family, helping us survive the year financially.

On May 8, 2010, we were celebrating my dad's birthday when we received a phone call from my dad's surgeon informing us that the growth was stage IV cancer. With the shocking news, we began our search for treatment options and, by God's grace, we ended up at Duke University Brain Tumor Center.

God has been right by our side along this journey. A Bible verse He has used to comfort and encourage me along the way is Philippians 4:13 which says, "I can do all things through Christ who strengthens me." I'm not sure how all this is going to end, but I am putting my faith in Christ to pull us through this battle with cancer!

# From Mallory...

MY FIRST REACTION TO THE NEWS that my dad had brain cancer was fear! This year has been scary and unforgettable in so many ways. For example, God has shown me that He will be with me no matter what the circumstances of my life look like. God has taught me that no matter how horrible things are, I need to trust Him because He promises to give me the strength I need to fight through the rough times and He will help me make it through whatever life brings my way.

In the end, I've realized that this journey turned out to be less devastating than I thought it would be. I have learned so much about God and how to trust Him more in every area of my life and every day of my life. God's word is full of promises and if I will read His word and believe it, I can make it through the toughest of times!

Chapter One

# The Journey...

*"Go in peace. The LORD is watching over the journey you are going on." Judges 18:6 HCSB*

Mirriam-Webster defines the word "journey" as an act or instance of traveling from one place to another. I have come to define the word "journey" as life itself. On this journey of life, God desires to lead us down various paths that take us, step by step, deeper into His heart. This is the true prize of life...to find and know and dwell in the depths of God's heart!

My journey has taken me on a very strenuous and unfamiliar path lately. On April 28, 2010, my husband, Mike, was diagnosed with a very deadly form of brain cancer. Our lives were turned upside down, needless to say, and we have since journeyed to a whole new level of faith and understanding of God's love. Over the course of this journey, I have scaled mountains, hidden in crevices, nearly fallen off cliffs into pits of fear, doubt, and dread...each time being rescued by the love and grace of God. I've rested in meadows of peace and stood on mountain tops so high I felt as if I could literally lift my hands and touch heaven. I've felt lost at times, surrounded by mighty oaks of loneliness and isolation. At other times, I've sought the refuge of a dark cave to just escape and distract myself from the reality of life. Regardless of the scenery and circumstances...God was always there!

Each step of this journey, each challenge, and each glorious, frightening, or dull sight has brought me deeper into the heart of God. There has not been a single moment that He has not been there with me; never a circumstance that I felt forsaken or abandoned. God has been a refuge in times of trouble, a place to rest when I have been weary, and the object of my praise in moments of glory and moments of deep pain.

I will admit it has taken stubborn determination and mountain moving faith to believe in and trust God's sovereignty, love, and grace throughout this phase of my life's journey. No doubt, there have been times that I have failed my Savior, but He has never failed me! He has taken me down unfamiliar paths, causing me to be more attentive to each step in order to not fall, and He has faithfully made the rough places smooth and taken me by the hand when I have stumbled. He has led each step of the way to this new and unknown place (Isaiah 42:16).

He has carried me when I felt like I could not manage to take another step. This is true of all of us – God desires to lead us to the very depths of His heart even if it requires crossing treacherous terrain and unfamiliar trails. Thankfully, He is leading us to a place where the distractions of life and the lies of the enemy are nowhere to be found. A place, like no other, where we can experience His perfect and pure love that casts out all our fears.

This has been the most difficult leg of my life's journey – watching my husband battle brain cancer and fight for his life – watching my children live in fear of losing their daddy. Nevertheless, it has been the most blessed path I have walked. I have found so many treasures along the way – treasures that moths and rust cannot destroy – treasures that cannot be stolen or taken from me – treasures I will cherish in my heart as long as my life journey continues – treasures that reflect the very heart of God.

Thank you for joining me on this journey! My prayer is that you will also discover these treasures for yourself. When you seek Him with all your heart, you will find Him (Jeremiah 29:13). When we call out to Him and long to know and follow Him, He will show us amazing things about Himself and His glorious plan for our lives (Jeremiah 33:3)...things that we could never ask for or imagine...things that we will never know and discover by just skimming the surface. He reveals these treasures as we journey into the depths of His heart. This is definitely the road less traveled...but maybe that is what makes it such a beautiful, peaceful place!

My hope is that God will somehow place this book in the hands of someone in need of encouragement...someone who needs to see the glory of God and feel His tender touch...someone who can somehow relate to what my family has gone through and be strengthened and given hope by reading about our journey and how God has carried us...someone who is caring for or loves someone who is going through a crisis and can glean lessons and insights from our writings that might help them support, encourage, and minister to others. Regardless of what the crisis might be...the answer to your need is the same as ours...the love of God revealed in Jesus and His powerful, healing love. Ultimately, my goal in writing this book is to glorify God and display His marvelous grace and love to all who read it!

# How it all began....April 28, 2010

It was a calm evening. I was home recuperating from shoulder surgery. The kids were at church and Mike came home to eat a bite before going to an appointment to have an MRI on his head. He had been having sinus problems for several weeks (probably more like months), and after not responding to antibiotic treatment, his doctor decided he needed to have an MRI to rule out a more serious issue. At that point, our definition of "a more serious issue" paled in comparison to what we were about to discover. I offered to go with him, but he calmly said, "I really don't think you need to. I will be back in about an hour. No big deal." So we thought!

The kids had gotten home from church and were making themselves some mac and cheese. Mike called to inform me that the MRI technician had spotted a lesion on his brain and had sent him straight to the ER and that I needed to find someone to bring me up there so we could figure out exactly what was going on and what was going to happen. "Lesion...what does that mean?", I asked. My stomach instantly twisted into knots and I felt like I was going to throw up. I knew exactly what that meant and it wasn't good!

I hung up the phone and took a deep breath. *O.K.*, I thought to myself, *stay calm! Get the kids squared away and then deal with things one step at a time.* Thankfully, the kids were able to stay with a neighbor and, despite Mike's objections, I drove myself (one armed as I was) to the hospital. When I got there, Mike was flat on his back and had been instructed not to sit up. They had already given him a dose of steroids to help combat the swelling in his brain. Mike was calm and cracking jokes. I was just trying to keep from throwing up. I finally got the nerve to ask the doctor, "So...should we be concerned?" I am sure

16

he was thinking, *Are you kidding me...lady...your husband has a mass the size of a super ball in his head and you are asking me if you should be concerned?*, but he was very kind and gracious and simply said, "Yes, it is very serious." Bummer, I was hoping for an answer that would feed into my denial, not slap me in the face and wake me to the reality of this nightmare!

Being the super woman that I am (in my mind at least) I had told friends that I was OK and did not need anyone to come to the ER. However, only a real friend knows when to respect your wishes and when to ignore your stubbornness. Thankfully, we have some wonderful friends who rushed to be by our side despite my decline of their offer to do so. In fact, when I called one of them to give an update, she said, "So, is it OK that we are at the interstate exit for the hospital or should we go home?" (with a hint of humor of course...they had no intention of going home!). About the time they arrived, an ambulance had been ordered to transport Mike to another hospital that could better meet his needs. In hindsight, this was the grace of God covering us and meeting our needs. It just so happened that the hospital we were at was experiencing cutbacks and had lost much of its staff. Otherwise, Mike would have been treated by doctors who were much less qualified and I am sure we would not have had the sense to seek a second opinion due to our state of shock. In the end, God placed us exactly where we needed to be and in the care of a wonderful neurosurgeon.

Within a matter of a couple of hours, Mike went from being in the MRI machine to being transported and into a room at the University of Tennessee Medical Center. It was like being in a modern day version of the Wizard of Oz. A storm had hit and we found ourselves in a strange, unknown place wondering how in the world we could get back to our calm, simple life. Well...we are still in Oz and this is no dream...it is real...and we are living it!

As you might expect, we did not sleep a wink that night. The next morning, Dr. Miller, an angel sent in the form of a neurosurgeon, came to visit Mike and give us his first impressions and recommended

17

plan of treatment. He insisted that he could not give us a final diagnosis and prognosis until the tumor had been removed and a pathology report had been received. However, it was obvious that he suspected what we had feared. Let's just say, the words malignant and stage IV were mentioned and not in order to assure us that they could be ruled out. We left the hospital later that day fairly certain of what we were in for...a long, bumpy, scary ride. That was Thursday and Mike would return to UT Medical Center on Monday to undergo a craniotomy to remove the tumor...after a long weekend of little sleep and much prayer!

The most difficult thing about leaving the hospital to head home was the thought of having to talk to our children. I mean, is there a good way or a proper way to tell a 12 and 14 year old that their dad might have brain cancer? This was definitely the most difficult thing I have yet to do as a mother. We hit our knees and begged God to give us wisdom and the perfect words to say...not too much, but not too little. We prayed that the kids would turn to God for strength and not doubt Him or be angry at Him for allowing this to happen. God answered our prayers and we made it through the most emotional conversation we have ever had to have with our children. They were so strong and God was (and continues to be) faithful to guard their hearts and minds. We told them only what we KNEW...dad had a tumor in his brain...it had to be removed...and God is in control and He loves us very much! We did not speculate or talk about the what if's or unknowns. We were not going to lie to them, but we also knew that their little minds could not handle information that would only lead to more questions without answers.

Family and friends surrounded us immediately! Mike's mom and dad drove in from Indiana and my mom and dad and one of my sisters drove in from Texas. Our church family encircled us with a hedge of love, prayers, and support. Although I know she will not be happy, I am going to have to give a shout out to Micki (and her husband Mike). I honestly do not know what we would have done without them. Micki is the queen of stepping up to the plate, and when she does, she hits it out of the park! Mike and Micki were there supporting us from that dreadful night in the ER. I know my sanity was maintained by knowing that they were there to catch me and anything else that might fall. Everyone needs a Mike and Micki in their life. And then there are Kent and Amy. I think Kent took all this harder than I did. Talk about a true friend. He has been there for Mike in ways that I could not. Everyone needs a Kent and Amy dynamic duo, too! Their love and compassion and faith are like a warm cozy blanket and when they are around, you just feel the love!

Sunday morning at church was one of those moments we will never forget. It was a beautiful picture of the body of Christ...an expression of God's love that could not be scripted by anyone other than the Holy Spirit. Hundreds gathered around Mike at the front of our worship center to show their love and support and to pray for him. It was one of those moments you want to go on and never end. As we stood there in the midst of so many brothers and sisters in Christ, we felt completely surrounded and immersed in God's love. Nevertheless, Sunday came to an end and the reality of what lie ahead could no longer be pushed to the back of our minds. Monday arrived with a great sense of peace. We were ready!

The remainder of this book is a glimpse into the amazing journey God has taken us on and the many lessons we have learned through our suffering. We were encouraged early on to set up a caringbridge website to help keep our friends and family informed about Mike's health and progress and to share prayer requests. Our journal posts quickly turned into an outlet for me and a great form or therapy! Along the way, we were continually asked if we would consider publishing the journal entries. One day, I jokingly told Mike, "If one more person asks if we are going to publish our caringbridge journals, we just might have to do it!" Well...I guess you know what happened! Once we began to think about publishing our journey, God began impressing upon our hearts the desire to establish a ministry to help families traveling on similar journeys. You can read more about the

Isaiah 42:16 Ministry and our mission in the **About the Author** section of this book or go to www.Isaiah4216ministry.org.

It has been quite a ride! There have been moments I have been scared to death...moments I have skipped along with a smile on my face and a song of praise in my heart...moments I thought I was going to be completely taken over by anxiety and the uncertainty of even the next day. In the end, though, I can say without a doubt that this has been a journey that I would never give up if given the chance to turn back the hands of time and make this all go away. Honestly! Each painful, dreadful moment has been worth the joy and blessings that have come from the chance to know and rest in the heart of the One who loves us more than we can comprehend. As Job said...we have heard about Him but now our eyes have seen (Job 42:5). We have heard others talk about seeing the glory of God in ways that we could never truly understand. We have heard others talk about experiencing peace in the midst of trials in ways that we just could not fully comprehend. But now...our eyes have seen the glory of God like never before...we have felt His touch like never before...we have experienced His peace like never before...we have rested in His love like never before. Now, our eyes have seen...and we would not trade that for anything in this world! HE is truly the only thing that will satisfy the longings and desires of our heart! HE is our treasure...our prize...our joy!

I know of no better way to describe our experience and what we have gained than to echo Paul's words in Philippians 3:7-14. As Paul points out, there is no greater way to fully experience the glory, love, and grace of God than going through some type of suffering. Suffering brings us to the point of complete and utter desperation and reliance on God's resurrection power. It is during these times of suffering that we understand the full accomplishment of the cross and we can wholeheartedly say...death where is your sting? Nothing can separate me from the love of God which is in Christ my Lord!

*"I once thought these things were valuable, but now I consider them worthless because of what Christ has done. Yes, everything else is*

20

*worthless when compared with the infinite value of knowing Christ Jesus my Lord. For his sake I have discarded everything else, counting it all as garbage, so that I could gain Christ and become one with him. I no longer count on my own righteousness through obeying the law; rather, I become righteous through faith in Christ. For God's way of making us right with himself depends on faith. I want to know Christ and experience the mighty power that raised him from the dead. I want to suffer with him, sharing in his death, so that one way or another I will experience the resurrection from the dead! I don't mean to say that I have already achieved these things or that I have already reached perfection. But I press on to possess that perfection for which Christ Jesus first possessed me. No, dear brothers and sisters, I have not achieved it, but I focus on this one thing: Forgetting the past and looking forward to what lies ahead, I press on to reach the end of the race and receive the heavenly prize for which God, through Christ Jesus, is calling us."*
*Philippians 3:7-14 NLT*

And so...we press on!

# *Your Story...*

Take a few moments to write about your personal journey. Where is God leading you at this moment? Are you going through a trial of your own or do you know someone who is...someone you might be able to encourage or comfort? How is God revealing himself to you through your current circumstances? How will you respond?

Chapter Two

# *Facing Our Giant...*

*"All those gathered here will know that it is not by sword or spear that the LORD saves..." 1 Samuel 17:47*

The days leading up to Mike's surgery were surreal.  I am not sure if I was numb, in denial, or in shock.  Thankfully, there was a lot of action around our house and a lot of details to take care of in order to get ready for surgery.  There were moments when we had nothing to say and just sat in silence, and there were other times that we consoled the other as they wept.  I knew Mike needed to have the freedom to express himself, but it was difficult for me to hear him express his fears and emotions.  He talked about his deep sadness at the thought of not being around to see the kids grow up...to see them graduate...to walk Mallory down the aisle...to see Davis grow into a man and lead his own family and follow God's plan for his life.  There were times I just had to tell him that I could not take it; that I could not listen to him express those fears.  There were other times I would just sit silently and listen, knowing I had no words of wisdom or comfort to offer that would really make a difference or ease his pain.

Then, there were the moment we took our trips down memory lane.  These were sweet times that drew our hearts closer and closer together.  There is nothing like a potentially terminal illness to clear out the cobwebs and open your eyes to the beauty of your life and the gift of love you share with others, especially your spouse.  I ached for Mike and would have given anything to have taken his place.  He is such a godly, giving man who does not deserve to feel the pain and heartache that he was feeling.  I felt so helpless and so desperate to find a way to fix this, but I couldn't fix things.  I could only love him and support him in whatever way he needed.

I wish I could provide a fool proof, step-by-step guide for how to deal with a crisis like cancer, but I cannot.  Such a guide does not exist.  Every journey is different.  However, there are a few "musts" that I believe are necessary for anyone who has come face-to-face with the reality that life has forever changed due to an unexpected crisis such as cancer, the loss of a loved one, divorce, etc. Fix your eyes on Jesus! Trust Him stubbornly and refuse effuse overtaken by doubt and the lies of the enemy! Accept the changes that have come and determine to see how God plans to use them for your good and His glory. Take things one day at a time and resist the temptation to focus on the "what if's", "if only's", and all the other unknowns. Cling to the hope you have due to God's great love and faithfulness. He will not leave you or forsake you!

Here are our initial journal entries to our caringbridge site and a glimpse into the first few days that followed that dreadful Wednesday night in the ER.

## Sharing the news...

O.K. So...here is what we know so far...Mike has a tumor a bit bigger than a golf ball on the front left lobe of his brain. It has been confirmed that the small mass was not just a picture of his entire brain as I had hoped and suspected (humor is good medicine). The neurosurgeon, Dr. Miller, suspects, but will not confirm, that it is a glioblastoma (GBM) primary brain tumor which is a malignant brain tumor that originated in the brain (as opposed to a tumor that has metastasized from somewhere else in his body). We will not know anything for sure until we receive the pathology report after the surgery on Monday. Long-term treatment (beyond removing it) will depend on the stage of the tumor. Anything over a stage 2 will require aggressive radiation and chemotherapy. It is our impression that Dr. Miller is anticipating a stage III or IV. We are home now and Mike is fine, just having headaches and some short-term memory issues (nothing major).

Mike will have a stealth MRI (doesn't that sound cool) on Saturday morning and surgery is scheduled for Monday at 1pm at UT Medical Center. The surgery will probably take about 4 to 5 hours. He will be in ICU for a day and then stay in the hospital approximately 2 or 3 more days. The pathology report could come back in a few days or up to 10 days. Radiation will not start until his surgical site heals which should take at least two weeks. BUT...we are praying BIG and not even penciling that in on our calendars.

In anticipation of surgery, Mike decided he wanted me to buzz his hair short...really short! That was quite a sight...me with my right arm in a sling trying to buzz his hair (keep in mind that I am right handed). Mike says he is still as handsome and studly as ever; however, he thinks that this new look (shaved head and soul patch) might bump him up a notch on the stud-o-meter...we'll see!

We feel hemmed in and completely surrounded by God's amazing, sufficient grace. When our bubble of denial was burst by the doctor, our Rock was there to catch us and we are standing firmly on all the promises tucked in our hearts! His grace is sufficient! His strength is made perfect in our weakness! He will never leave us or forsake us! His sweet, perfect peace does surpass all understanding! He provides our every need according to His glorious riches in Christ. That is the abbreviated list! We will keep you posted as the days pass.

## *An unfamiliar path...*

*"I will lead the blind by a way they did not know, I will guide them on paths they have not known; I will turn darkness to light in front of them, and rough places into level ground. This is what I will do for them, and I will not foresake them."* Isaiah 42:16 HCSB

This verse has been one that God has placed in our hearts over the past few days. It speaks volumes to us. First of all, it reminds us that this is a path that God has chosen for us! And we will choose to follow (like we have a choice). Next, it reminds us that, although the path He illuminates may look scary and hard, it is safer and more certain than any other path. This is the path, and the only path, that will lead us to His perfect peace. We will not look to the left or to the right, but only straight ahead into God's perfect light – a light that comes from the glow of His amazing love for us.

Today's devotion in *My Utmost For His Highest[1]* reads "It is impossible for us to have living, vital intercession unless we are perfectly and completely sure of God...Vital intercession leaves you with neither the time nor the inclination to pray for your own sad and pitiful self'".

As you go before God's throne today on Mike's behalf, go in faith and pray for His perfect will to be done. That is what Mike and I want deep down inside. Our God is a God who can and still does do

26

miracles. There will be many miracles along this journey and they will all have a purpose...not to answer our sad pitiful cries, but to make Him famous in this world. We will try to send out an update to let you all know exactly when the surgery begins. It is scheduled for 1pm.

*"But we have this treasure in jars of clay to show that this all-surpassing power is from God and not from us. We are hard pressed on every side, but not crushed; perplexed, but not in despair; persecuted, but not abandoned; struck down, but not destroyed. We always carry around in our body the death of Jesus, so that the life of Jesus may also be revealed in our body."* (II Cor. 4:7-10;

This is our prayer!

## Mission: tumor removal...

Well...needless to say, we are having a big ole celebration down here. Surgery is done and Dr. Miller was pleased with how the tumor came out – intact and fairly easy to remove.  It has settled down a bit and I am sure hospital security is thankful for that! It has been a happenin' place. We bypassed the surgery lounge and took over the main lobby of the hospital all afternoon. There was much laughing and sweet fellowship! The whole day flew by in mach speed compared to the past hour and a half spent waiting not-so-patiently to see Mike. Due to a shift change, we are having to wait a bit longer for him to get to a room. I will write more once I get to see Mike!

YAY...we finally got to go up and see Mike. He looks GREAT!!!! He was very alert and talking. I asked him if he knew what time it was and he said, "there's a clock right there on the wall." He was propped up and able to reach over to the little bed side tray and get his cup of water and was sipping through a straw. I AM AMAZED...they just opened his head and took out part of his brain!  I did not expect to find him propped up in his bed talking and sipping water!

It took Mike all of about 10 minutes to be worn out. Davis, Mallory and a few others got to go up and see him, and then we headed out to give him time to rest. He will have an MRI at some point tonight to check for swelling and bleeding and a lot of poking and prodding so PLEASE pray (If you are still up) that he can relax and get some rest. As for where we go from here...it all depends on the pathology report. Keep those prayers going!

*"I have seen you in the sanctuary and beheld your power and your glory. Because your love is better than life, my lips will glorify you. I will praise you as long as I live, and in your name I will lift up my hands. My soul will be satisfied as with the richest of foods; with singing lips my mouth will praise you. "* Psalm 63:2-5

We have seen His glory over the past few days in ways we've never seen before. Knowing and experiencing His great LOVE is better than life and anything this life has to offer. He has truly satisfied our souls these past few days. I cannot begin to explain it...I only hope and pray that you experience it for yourselves. To be tucked into the Lord, within the shelter of His wings (Psalm 91) is the most beautiful thing I have ever felt. I hope and pray that nothing will ever take the place of this longing to just BE HERE in this place...within the shelter of His wings and wrapped in His love!

## *Miracle number one...*

I just got done seeing Mike. I chose to leave the room so Mike would stop talking and rest! It is so crazy and I just still cannot believe that Mike is so alert after having brain surgery. He is better off right now than I was after having my shoulder replaced a few weeks ago. Of course he is on a healthy dose of steroids which have him pretty juiced up...not to mention the pain killers.

When I got here Dr. Miller (the neurosurgeon) was in the room. They were both talking and smiling. He reassured me that the surgery was the ultimate success and could not have gone better from a tumor removal standpoint. He did not see any tentacles which is good; however, he also confirmed that there is the potential that there are microscopic cells that were not removed. The likelihood of that depends on the pathology and grade/stage of the tumor so that is where our prayers need to be focused now. Unfortunately, with this type of cancer, even the smallest of cells can somehow find a way to survive and thrive. Best case scenario is that all of the cancer cells were removed. Even though the surgery was a great success, the surgeon said there is no way for him to even speculate about the prognosis from what he saw. We will take the good news and be content for now! Waiting on the pathology report will no doubt be difficult. We are trusting that the Lord will take our thoughts captive and keep our eyes fixed on Him.

So...phase one was miraculous and now we need to pray for miracle number two! He is a lamp unto our feet illuminating only a step or two at a time. So, we take the next step fully trusting that our feet will land firmly even though we cannot fully see where this journey is taking us.

*Lord, Jesus, thank You for being You. YOU are our peace...not the good news we have gotten. YOU are our hope...not the wonderful doctors and medicine that we have access to. YOU are our strength...not the hundreds of people who are surrounding us (although we are so glad they are here). YOU are the reason we sing! We love You and we thank You from the bottom of our hearts. May Your glory shine and may all who hear this story see Your marvelous grace and love - not just Your love for us, but Your deep love for them, too! You long to lavish Your love and grace on us, but we often foolishly choose to seek things that gratify and satisfy our flesh rather than the longings of our soul. You and You alone are the only thing that will truly bring our hearts peace and contentment. We love You!*

# *Waiting in hope...*

      We had a great day. I spent most of the day in the room with Mike. He is doing GREAT. They got him up and he sat in a chair for several hours. I stayed until about 7pm and they still had not moved him to his room. He was cleared to go early in the day, but for some reason they never got him moved. He finally talked me into leaving so he would not worry about me and be able to get some rest. He tries to sleep but is not really able to. That is probably from the steroids. Amazingly, he is not in a lot of pain. He is getting pretty swollen on the left side of his face. Mallory says he looks like Squidword from Sponge Bob. Not sure Mike took that as a compliment...ha! It really is not that bad. Oh, and Mallory really wanted to touch his face to see if it felt squishy. Oh, Lord, we have to laugh!!!!!

As I write this journal entry, my heart is singing Psalm 33:1-22...

> *"Sing joyfully to the LORD, you righteous;*
> *it is fitting for the upright to praise him.*
> *Praise the LORD with the harp;*
> *make music to him on the ten-stringed lyre.*
> *Sing to him a new song;*
> *play skillfully, and shout for joy.*
> *For the word of the LORD is right and true;*
> *he is faithful in all he does.*
> *The LORD loves righteousness and justice;*
> *the earth is full of his unfailing love.*
> *By the word of the LORD were the heavens made,*
> *their starry host by the breath of his mouth.*
> *He gathers the waters of the sea into jars;*
> *he puts the deep into storehouses.*
> *Let all the earth fear the LORD;*
> *let all the people of the world revere him.*
> *For he spoke, and it came to be;*
> *he commanded, and it stood firm.*

*The LORD foils the plans of the nations;*
*he thwarts the purposes of the peoples.*
*But the plans of the LORD stand firm forever,*
*the purposes of his heart through all generations.*
*Blessed is the nation whose God is the LORD,*
*the people he chose for his inheritance.*
*From heaven the LORD looks down and sees all mankind;*
*from his dwelling place he watches all who live on earth-*
*he who forms the hearts of all,*
*who considers everything they do.*
*No king is saved by the size of his army;*
*no warrior escapes by his great strength.*
*A horse is a vain hope for deliverance;*
*despite all its great strength it cannot save.*
*But the eyes of the LORD are on those who fear him,*
*on those whose hope is in his unfailing love,*
*to deliver them from death and keep them alive in famine.*
*We wait in hope for the LORD;*
*he is our help and our shield.*
*In him our hearts rejoice,*
*for we trust in his holy name.*
*May your unfailing love rest upon us, O LORD,*
*even as we put our hope in you"*

He is such a wonderful God!

## *Walking by faith...*

You will not believe this, but Mike is home and resting in his favorite chair. YES...I said Mike is HOME. He was cleared to go home and they said he would probably rest better at home than at the hospital. I could not agree more given that Monday night he had no sleep and an MRI at 2:30 a.m. and then he was transferred to his regular room at 3:30 a.m. this morning. Wow...less than 48 hours after brain surgery and we are home.

31

Now, our focus is on rest! We will probably turn the phones off and hibernate for a few days. Please continue to pray concerning the pathology report. We are praying for God's glory to shine! We need your prayers and we are so thankful that we KNOW we can count on them. The prayers of the righteous are powerful and effective! Boy are we happy we have so many saints on our side!!!!

Today, I am clinging to Proverbs 3:5-6, leaning not on my own understanding, but claiming all I know to be true about my God and trusting FULLY that He WILL direct our paths. Jeremy Camp's song *I Will Walk BY Faith*[2] resonates in my mind and heart right now! We will walk by faith even though we cannot see because this broken road prepares His will for us!!!! We will continue to walk by faith...

## *A few good laughs...*

We had a few good laughs yesterday and I just wanted to share a couple. First of all, Mike has been going crazy not being able to see. The left side of his face is still pretty swollen plus his glasses would touch his stitches so he is not able to wear them. I thought it might work if we just took off the left ear piece so I went upstairs and grabbed his glasses and went to work on them. When he put them on they were all wapper-jawed on his face and he said that the surgery or steroids must be messing up his vision because he couldn't see clearly. I wish you could have seen him (he wouldn't let me post a picture). It was hysterical!!!!!! We were laughing so hard. Well...then it hit me, Davis and Mike's glasses are almost identical. I had taken Davis' glasses apart!

Here is another good one. Last night Mike was sleeping in the recliner in our bedroom, I was in the bed, and Davis was on an air mattress in our room. Mike was up several times (I was up with him), Davis was restless, talking in his sleep and making all kinds of noises due to his allergies. Finally, at one point, Davis got up and was roaming around our room trying to find the bathroom, still half asleep. I got up and got him to the restroom. When I came back out Mike was cracking up and said, "It is a real three ring circus in here!" To which I replied,

"Yeah...all we are missing is a giant great dane!" (referring to our dog Dooku).

Believe it or not, we both feel pretty rested...that was probably the best sleep we have had in a week. Mike is up this morning and sitting at the kitchen table eating some breakfast. Please remember to pray for his back. He is feeling a bit stiff and sitting around a lot seems to make his back problems worse. On the other hand, being up and moving around a lot wears him out. So...pray that we find a good balance and that God places His healing touch on Mike's back.

## The dawn brings new light....and JOY!

*"Satisfy us in the morning with your unfailing love, that we may sing for joy and be glad all our days." Psalm 90:14*

It is in the stillness of the night that our minds are most aware of the reality of this journey. Kind of like when you are camping and get settled in for the night and begin to hear the sounds of nature that aren't so obvious during the light of day. But when morning comes, the light and beauty of day seems to distract us from our fears and brings joy back to our hearts.

God's love has a way of doing that. When there is darkness, our senses seem to be more aware of the unknown which can be frightening, but when light comes and we are able to see, then the fear subsides and we feel more at peace. God's love and faithfulness shine a great light into our hearts filling them with great confidence, peace, and JOY! But we must choose to let the light in! We must choose to dwell in the light, and when we find ourselves in a dark place (maybe we are lured there by our fears or worries), we must run back into His glorious light or ask Him to bring that light to us if we are too weary to carry ourselves there. He will never leave us or forsake us! He comes, in glorious light, when we call! Darkness is merely the absence of light! In Him, there is no darkness. Even tucked tightly within His wings there is always a comforting glow! Praying that YOU are filled with the JOY that comes from living in His glorious light! He loves you!

Psalm 96:1-13
*"Sing to the LORD a new song;*
*sing to the LORD, all the earth.*
*Sing to the LORD, praise his name;*
*proclaim his salvation day after day.*
*Declare his glory among the nations,*
*his marvelous deeds among all peoples.*
*For great is the LORD and most worthy of praise;*
*he is to be feared above all gods.*
*For all the gods of the nations are idols,*
*but the LORD made the heavens.*
*Splendor and majesty are before him;*
*strength and glory are in his sanctuary.*
*Ascribe to the LORD, O families of nations,*
*ascribe to the LORD glory and strength.*
*Ascribe to the LORD the glory due his name;*
*bring an offering and come into his courts.*
*Worship the LORD in the splendor of his holiness;*
*tremble before him, all the earth.*
*Say among the nations, "The LORD reigns."*
*The world is firmly established, it cannot be moved;*
*he will judge the peoples with equity.*
*Let the heavens rejoice, let the earth be glad;*
*let the sea resound, and all that is in it;*
*let the fields be jubilant, and everything in them.*
*Then all the trees of the forest will sing for joy;*
*they will sing before the LORD, for he comes,*
*he comes to judge the earth.*
*He will judge the world in righteousness*
*and the peoples in his truth."*

We are basking in His glory...

# *Faith to persevere...*

Good morning and Happy Mother's Day to all you moms! It is the perfect Mother's Day here in TN -sunny, a little chill in the air, flowers blooming, birds singing. I am glad Mother's Day is in the spring!

Mike woke up with a skip in his step today. Mr. Chatty Kathy! That is good to see! He had a fabulous birthday yesterday and appreciated all the b-day wishes...and to top it off his girls won their last soccer game and were able to send him a video greeting! He loves those girls!

God continues to speak so tenderly to our hearts. This morning's Oswald Chambers[1] reading is titled *Faith To Persevere*. I love this..."Faith is not some weak and pitiful emotion, but is a strong and vigorous confidence built on the fact that God is holy love. And even though you cannot see Him right now and cannot understand what He is doing, you know Him. Disaster occurs in your life when you lack the mental composure that comes from establishing yourself on the eternal truth that God is holy love. Faith is the supreme effort of your life - throwing yourself with abandon and total confidence upon God...The real meaning of eternal life is a life that can face anything it has to face without wavering. If we take this view, life will become one great romance - a glorious opportunity of seeing wonderful things all the time."

Those words are so true, whether we choose to believe them or not. God's word/truth stand no matter what we choose to believe. Agreeing with God is the ultimate victory in this life...agreeing that He is who He says He is...that we are who He says we are...that He can do what He says He can do...that He is holy, pure love and that we exist because of His great love. Praying that you may know, today and every day, how deep and high and wide God's love is for you and that His love will consume your heart and satisfy your deepest desires! We are feeling the love...

"But God showed his great love for us by sending Christ to die for us while we were still sinners." Romans 5:8 NLT

# Trying to be still...

Good morning, everyone. Just wanted to give you a quick update. Mike is doing great!!! He is getting stronger every day and having to use very little pain medicine if any. He is sleeping well, too! His back is holding up but quite stiff and sore. He has been able to do some of his exercises and stretches so maybe that will help. We should be able to post later tonight or tomorrow morning concerning the pathology report. Thank you all for continuing to pray for us during this "holding pattern".

*"The LORD himself will fight for you. Just stay calm." Exodus 14:14 NLT*

*"Be still before the LORD and wait patiently for him;..." Psalm 37:7*

*"...Be still, and know that I am God;..." Psalm 46:10*

We are so thankful that Jesus is calming the storms that hit our hearts and toss us to and fro. With just a word from Jesus...the storm dies down and we are completely calm.

# The results are in...

The long awaited news is here. Let me just get right to it. The tumor was a stage 4 primary brain tumor (giant cell glioblastoma multiforme). Mike will begin radiation and chemo as soon as his incision heals. We see the oncologist on May 18 and his first treatment is scheduled for May 28.

We are stunned and shocked by the news, but God is still on His throne and we are placing all of this in His hands. My first reaction was that all H--- had broken loose, but God quickly changed that to all heaven has broken loose! He fights for us!!!! One of the Scriptures God took us to early on in this journey was Isaiah 42:16 - *"I will lead the blind*

36

*by ways they have not known, along unfamiliar paths I will guide them; I will turn the darkness into light before them and make the rough places smooth. These are the things I will do; <u>I will not forsake them."</u>*
(emphasis mine)

These words are true and they remain a great source of hope, giving us great peace. He is Jehovah Rapha- the God who heals. He is El Shaddai - our all sufficient God. He is El Roi - the God who sees us. He is Elohim - the almighty God! He is who He says He is! He is the same God who parted the Red Sea, made the blind see and the lame walk. He is the same God who loved us so much, He sent His son to die in our place so that we might live with Him forever. His perfect love is casting out all our fears as we dwell in Him. When we dwell within the shelter of His great name, we find rest (Psalm 91). He is our strong tower, our refuge in times of trouble. He is the God who sings over us and delights in us. He is the God we love!

Thank you all for your prayers. We have been completely blown away and overwhelmed by your love and support!!!!!! We are so blessed! PLEASE, PLEASE, PLEASE don't stop. Pray for a miracle...for complete and total healing. God says we should ask in His name and according to His will. May His will be done...may all of this make Him famous in this world...a world who needs a loving God so desperately! Thank you for joining us on this journey! Buckle your seat belts! We will keep you posted!

# *Your Story...*

Is God leading you down an "unfamiliar path" right now? Are you walking by faith? If so...take some time to record some of the ways God has shown Himself faithful through your circumstances. If not...take some time to identify any "giants" that might be threatening your ability to surrender to and trust God's plan for your life – even if it includes painful, frightening circumstances. Or...maybe you need wisdom on how to encourage a friend who is on an "unfamiliar path". Stop here and pray...ask God to show you how He might use you to speak truth into this person's life...truth that can defeat the giant he or she is facing.

Chapter Three

# *Now What?*

*"Now if any of you lacks wisdom, he should ask God, who gives to all generously and without criticizing, and it will be given to him. But let him ask in faith without doubting. For the doubter is like the surging sea, driven and tossed by the wind." James 1:5-6 HCSB*

Mike actually received the results of the pathology report on May 8 (his birthday). We were not surprised. Dr. Miller had given us a pretty good indication that we could expect the tumor to be a stage IV GBM, but there was always hope that the results would prove otherwise. Now we had a new mission...beating this thing!

Of course, one of the first things we did when Mike got home from the hospital was to begin researching GBM brain tumors. WOW! This is not good! The prognosis for someone with this cancer is bleak. Over 50% die within one year, nearly 75% make it less than a year before the cancer returns, and only approximately 10% live past three years from the time of diagnosis. However, when God is involved, statistics don't mean squat! Our God is a mountain mover! He parts the seas, raises the dead, conquers sin, and saves the souls of man. He is in control of the outcome of this story! We are placing our faith and trust in Him and Him alone.

We were experiencing a whirlwind of emotions, decisions, and details. We had seen God do amazing things, and were experiencing His love and grace like never before. As we dove deeper into His heart, we saw glimpses of His glory that caused us to fall deeper and deeper in love with Him. We were discovering aspects of God's love that we would never know apart from this trial. We were experiencing His grace, His unmerited favor, in ways that defy explanation. "Amazing grace, how sweet the sound. Amazing love now flowing down, from hands and feet that were nailed to a tree...as grace flows down and covers me." (*Grace Flows Down*[3]). He so freely gives this grace through the One He sent (Jesus) to shed His blood in order that we might be free to experience the grace He longs to lavish on us (Ephesians 1:8). What a great and glorious mystery this is! May all who read this and hear our story be amazed by the love, grace, and glory of God! To Him be all the glory and honor and praise! Now that we know where we are, it is time to move on!

These next few journal entries and remainder of this chapter describe the days spent trying to make decisions regarding the path we would choose for Mike's treatment protocol. Talk about seeking God like never before. This was an agonizing yet supernaturally peaceful part of the journey. We were hyper focused and tuned into God's voice like never before. We knew He was for us and not against us, and we knew we could trust the Holy Spirit to guide us along this leg of this unfamiliar path.

## Oh Happy Day!

It may seem like a little thing, but Mike was so excited to get his stitches out today!!!! He is a happy camper. The nurse said he is healing nicely so he should be on target to start treatments soon. This is a huge praise. Today was his first day out of the neighborhood since surgery. He was singing his freedom song! We stopped by the church to see everyone. That was so uplifting for Mike! He misses everyone! Then we went to lunch and to get an eye exam so he could get contacts. He is still a bit swollen on the side of his face and down near his ear making it difficult to wear his glasses. A new doo, contacts, and a gnarly scar...I have one handsome hubby!!!!!

We are hoping to speak with a doctor from Duke University this week. A friend of ours whose mother was diagnosed with GBM brain cancer has spoken with him regarding her mother's treatment and suggested that we contact him. We are hopeful and anxious to hear what he has to say. We are learning a great deal as we continue to read the latest research on the breakthrough treatment protocols that are being used to treat GBM's. Please pray that God will open doors and give us wisdom concerning Mike's treatment.

# A Short update...

Just a quick update. Mike is feeling GREAT! He is getting stronger every day and enjoying getting out a bit to run errands. He is outside right now watering the flowers. We got a phone call from Dr. Friedman at Duke this morning. Since Mike has already had surgery to remove the tumor, he is not the guy we really need to talk to so he forwarded our information to someone else and they will hopefully call Monday. We are hoping they can give us some insight concerning what treatment route to take. We see Dr. Stephen Miller from UT on Tuesday and are considering "interviewing" other oncologists here in town. There is actually a clinical trial going on at Thompson Cancer Survival Center in Knoxville that might be a good option. It incorporates standard treatment protocol plus a drug that has been used with patients who have recurring GBM tumors and this drug seems to be beneficial in these patients. The clinical trial is looking at whether or not it should be added to first round treatment. It is a randomized trial so Mike might get the drug or he might get a placebo. Regardless, he would get the standard radiation and chemo that is routinely used.

So...please pray that God will give us wisdom and direct our path to the best doctor and treatment option. This decision seems very overwhelming to us at times, but prayer and thanksgiving bring much peace as we remember all the ways we have seen God's hand move over the past few months and weeks.

Thanks for your continued love, support, encouragement, and prayers. Please don't discount how much your words strengthen us!!!! They are constant reminders of God's faithfulness and power! Praying that God moves in your life and blesses you as you travel this journey with us!!! We are resting in Him!

# *Update on doctors...*

Mike will see Dr. Stephen Miller at UT tomorrow and then we will talk to Thompson Cancer Center on Thursday. The clinical trial at Thompson is looking very promising and we are leaning in that direction. Please pray that we ask all the right questions and that God gives us peace about which path to take. We are clinging to Proverbs 3:5-6 like never before. We are not able to lean on our own understanding right now, because, well, we don't understand much of what is going on. Reading clinical mumbo jumbo can make your head spin and flat wear you out. BUT, things are starting to make sense and we are beginning to have a whole new level of optimism as we read some of the latest research and talk to medical professionals who deal with this stuff.

Please pray for the kids. We decided to send Dooku (our great dane that we adopted in November) back to the dane rescue to be adopted out to another family. This was such a hard decision, but we know that it is best. With Mike and I both struggling, we cannot take care of him like we need to, and we don't know when that might change. Dooku was getting really stressed out. He had been staying with the rescue temporarily and we went over to say "good-bye" this afternoon. That was tough! Especially for the kids. I am amazed by their courage and resilience. I know this can only come from God's protection and grace covering their hearts and minds.

Thanks for praying! Mike got a good nights sleep last night. I think that is the first night he has slept more than 4 hours since April 28. Hopefully, that will continue!

We will let you know what we find out on Tuesday and Thursday. Pray, Pray, Pray! We are expecting great things from our great God!!! He hears the prayers of His people and He answers our cries for help!

# Oncology visit #1...

We saw Dr. Stephen Miller at UT today. It was a good visit. We went in thinking we were about 90% sure that the clinical trial was the way to go. However, we gained some new information that makes us question that option. Rather than feeling confused, frustrated, and/or disappointed, we feel like God was definitely in control and providing us some very important information that we have not been able to discern through our own research efforts. The clinical trial looks very promising on the surface, but it is not clear cut and there are definitely some draw backs that we must continue to consider. We will address them when we meet with Dr. McCachren at Thompson Cancer Center on Thursday. We feel completely confident that God is going to illuminate the right path. What a relief to know that He is in control and sees the big picture!!!! How do people go through these trials without confidence in a loving God?

Mike slept well again last night! We left the house this morning and did not get home until 4:30 this afternoon and he was still going strong...I on the other hand am pooped! Oh...and I am not sure if I mentioned this, but when Mike had his eye exam last week the Dr. said his pressure was high and was concerned about glaucoma. He had that rechecked today and it was down...probably something related to the surgery. They will recheck it in 6 months just in case.

Please continue to pray with us for wisdom and discernment regarding treatment. Pray that Dr. McCachren will be open and straight forward with us and either confirm or legitimately deny Dr. Miller's concerns about the clinical trial and use of the drug Avastin as a first line of treatment.

I was reminded of this beautiful verse today..."I love the LORD because he hears my voice and my prayer for mercy. Because he bends down to listen, I will pray as long as I have breath!" Psalm 116:1-2 NLT.

What a beautiful image this verse conjures up in my mind. Like I would bend down to look eye-to-eye with my children when they are

44

expressing a concern, worry, need, or hurt, God bends down...comes down to our level...to look us in the eye...reassuring us that He hears our pleas for help and that He TRULY cares for us and feels our pain, or fear, or whatever is heavy on our heart. It is in those moments when we see God eye-to-eye that the words to the song, *How He Loves*[4], come to life... "all of the sudden I am unaware of these afflictions eclipsed by glory...and I realize just how beautiful you are and how great your affections are for me...OH HOW HE LOVES US!!!!"

Praying that you see God eye-to-eye today and that you know just how deeply He loves YOU!

## *Hitting our knees...*

Tomorrow is a BIG day. Please pray with us! We are seeing Dr. McCachren at Thompson Cancer Center at 1pm. This afternoon around 4:30, I e-mailed another doctor at Duke and by 6pm, he had called me. He is encouraging us to come to Duke where they are making great strides in research. They have a tremendous brain tumor research program there. We have been praying for God to clearly open a door. This one seems to have FLOWN open. Dr. Friedman at Duke is going to have someone call us tomorrow to talk more about what it would "look" like for us to go to Duke. You may remember that we had previously contacted a Dr. Friedman at Duke. Well...it turns out that there are two Dr. Friedman's associated with the Brain Tumor Center at Duke University. One is a neurosurgeon and one is a neuro-oncologist. The Dr. Friedman I talked to today is the guy we needed to speak to originally. Thank you, Lord for your sovereign hand!

*"If you need wisdom, ask our generous God, and he will give it to you. He will not rebuke you for asking. But when you ask him, be sure that your faith is in God alone. Do not waver, for a person with divided loyalty is as*

*unsettled as a wave of the sea that is blown and tossed by the wind."*
James 1:5-6 NLT

Trusting Him...

## *Perfect peace...*

*"You will keep in perfect peace all who trust in you, all whose thoughts are fixed on you! Trust in the LORD always, for the LORD GOD is the eternal Rock."* Isaiah 26:3-4 NLT

We have stubbornly trusted in our God and have determined to keep our minds steadfast on HIM even in the midst of this whirlwind of emotions. And, as He promised, He has kept us in PERFECT peace! Today was the day we had hoped it would be. Our visits with Dr. McCachren (oncologist at Thompson Cancer Center) and Dr. Scaperoth (Radiation Oncologist at Thompson) were outstanding!!!! Dr. McCachren encouraged us to pursue a visit at Duke, and he assured us that he would support whatever decision we made.  How refreshing!

We heard from Duke and are in the process of sending them all the information they need to evaluate Mike as a candidate for the clinical trial they have going on which is studying the efficacy of using Avastin with newly diagnosed GBM patients. Avastin is a promising drug used with recurrent/progressed GBM patients.  In many cases, when individuals have recurrent GBM tumors and are prescribed Avastin, it stops the progression of the tumors and they have increased longevity of life expectancy. It is hoped that Avastin will potentially prevent or postpone the recurrence of GBM tumors in individuals who have had a successful resection (tumor removal). It is complicated, but Avastin basically disrupts the blood flow to the tumor and it cannot thrive and grow like it normally does.  It may also be that the Avastin helps a larger quantity of the chemo drugs pass through the blood-brain barrier. From what we understand, some theories suggest that only a certain percentage of the chemo drug dosage taken actually passes through the blood-brain barrier to reach the brain. But don't quote me on that!

There is not a lot of hard data to support the use of Avastin in first line of treatment, but initial clinical trials are producing some positive data. The reason we are looking into Duke vs. Thompson is that Thompson's clinical trial is a double blind study which means they have a randomly assigned control group and those patients receive a placebo rather than the Avastin...no way to predict whether Mike would get the drug. Duke, however, has a one armed study meaning there is not a control group and everyone gets Avastin.

Mike and I are both praising God for directing our path and feel such perfect peace about where we are at this point! Thank you for interceding on our behalf! What a gift to be able to come boldly to the throne of grace! As I type this, I am thinking about Hebrew 10:23-25 *"Let us hold unswervingly to the hope we profess, for he who promised is faithful. And let us consider how we may spur one another on toward love and good deeds. Let us not give up meeting together, as some are in the habit of doing, but let us encourage one another—and all the more as you see the Day approaching."* We are clinging to the hope we have and all we know to be true of our wonderful, loving God and you all spur us on...encouraging us to stay strong and to believe God and trust Him completely! Hope...anxious expectation...not wishful thinking. We anxiously (in a good way) sit back with expectation as we wait to see God move and work in ways that only He can!

We are praying that God will expedite the preparation of all the information Duke needs in order for us to get an appointment next week. They will not even schedule an appointment until they receive medical records and the pathology slides to confirm that Mike is a candidate. We are waiting on UT to process and send the pathology slides to Duke. This is hard given that we are both "if you want something done right, do it yourself" type of people...if we could prepare pathology slides we would go down there and do it ourselves...ugh! Pray that Mike and I will endure this hurry up and wait time with peace and patience!

Oh...and one more praise...Dr. McCachren was very impressed with the post-surgery MRI and confirmed that the surgery was a huge success and added much hope to Mike's prognosis. We actually got to view the pre and post-op MRI's...OH MY GOODNESS...that thing was huge and there was so much swelling. I can see why the staff at Mercy North responded to the MRI the way they did...wow! It was cool to see! We are feeling extremely steadfast and strong as we move into this next phase and leg of our journey...

# *Your Story...*

Are you in need of answers?  Sometimes life can throw us a curveball...sometimes we stand at a cross road, paralyzed by the fear of making the wrong decision.  God is not a God of confusion!  He is not going to hang you out to dry!  He will not leave you stranded!  Take a few moments to record some of the areas of your life where you are in need of God's wisdom and direction, or pray for a friend who might be going through a crisis and ask the Lord to speak peace into their heart and mind.  In the book of Jeremiah, we are reminded that we have a heavenly Father who longs for us to seek Him and look to Him for answers.  By His Holy Spirit, He will guide us and give us the wisdom we need.  Ask and believe!

Chapter Four

# On The Right Path...

*"Trust in the LORD with all your heart, and do not rely on your own understanding; think about Him in all your ways, and He will guide you on the right paths." Proverbs 3:5-6 HCSB*

I cannot begin to explain the sense of relief we felt once we made a decision to travel to Duke University to explore the possibility of Mike participating in a clinical trial. This was both exciting and very scary. We realized we were taking a risk by choosing an option other than standard protocol for treatment. Unfortunately, the statistics related to standard treatment aren't good! We had done our research, consulted various medical professionals and we were ready to roll the dice so to speak.

Getting everything ready and in order for our visit to Duke was frantic! We were completely exhausted after chasing down records, pathology slides, and filling out paper work. Our heads were spinning! Poor Mike, he took the brunt of most of the chaos. I think he made three trips to UT Medical Center in one day and now he probably knows every hidden corridor in that facility. The records department knew him by name...lol!

At this point, it had not even been three full weeks since Mike's surgery. His incision was healing nicely and we were getting close to a treatment start date. In fact, we made it to Duke in the nick of time. It was mind boggling to step back and see all the intricate details that God had to orchestrate in order for us to come to this juncture of our journey. In order to participate in the Duke trial, Mike needed to start treatment by a certain post-surgery date. By the time we traveled to Duke, that date was fast approaching. It was also a push to get things squared away here in Knoxville with Thompson Cancer Survival Center in order for Mike to begin radiation treatments. However, we have an amazing, sovereign God, and He was faithful to make all the details fit together seamlessly. It was quite a spectacle to observe! The following journal entries tell the story of our trip to Duke and the preparation for treatments to begin...

## Duke bound...

Well...we are heading to Duke. After chasing down various medical reports and pathology slides, we were able to get an appointment set up today. We will head to Duke on Tuesday, next week, and see doctors on Wednesday and Thursday. It feels so good to have a plan in motion and to have come to a decision that we feel confident about. We will know more about a treatment plan after seeing the doctors at Duke. They will evaluate Mike to determine if he is a candidate for a clinical trial. If not, we will go with standard protocol. Either way, his radiation and chemo treatments (and any other medications) will be administered here in Knoxville at Thompson Cancer Center.

We have both taken a deep breath and released a huge sigh of relief today. I have to admit, Mike took the brunt of today's craziness running to the hospital to track down records and faxing them to Duke. I, on the other hand, made and answered phone calls from the spa chair while getting a pedicure...hey...a girl has to take a break now and then. I just needed to recharge and relax a bit! In exchange, I will prepare Mike a yummy dinner tonight and rub his tired feet and back!

Please continue to pray that the pathology slides get to Duke by Monday. Our appointments are pending their arrival. If they don't get there, we will have to postpone our appointments.

## *The Lord who heals...*

In Exodus 15, we meet Jehovah-Rapha - the LORD who heals us. We are introduced to this name for God through an interesting little story.

*"Then Moses led Israel from the Red Sea and they went into the Desert of Shur. For three days they traveled in the desert without finding water. When they came to Marah, they could not drink its water because it was bitter. (That is why the place is called Marah.) So the people grumbled against Moses, saying, "What are we to drink?" Then Moses cried out to the LORD, and the LORD showed him a piece of wood. He threw it into the water, **and the water became sweet**. There the LORD made a decree and a law for them, and there he tested them. He said, "If you listen*

51

*carefully to the voice of the LORD your God and do what is right in his eyes, if you pay attention to his commands and keep all his decrees, I will not bring on you any of the diseases I brought on the Egyptians, **for I am the LORD, who heals you**." (verses 22-26; emphasis added)*

There is a little treasure tucked away in these verses that might easily be overlooked. It is a beautiful picture of what happens to a life touched by God's love and grace when the challenges of this fallen world cause pain, heartache, and brokenness. Not only does God heal us of our brokenness (physical, spiritual, emotional), He replaces that brokenness (bitterness) with a sweetness that can only come from Him. As God has touched our lives thorough this circumstance, we have experienced a sweetness in our lives that was not there before. Yes...this is a priceless treasure...tucked away in a peculiar story that reveals God's true character. His word is full of these treasures and all the treasures and wisdom of God are HIDDEN in Christ (Colossians 2:3). Not hidden in order to keep them from us, but to draw us deeper into Him! God is such a creative God!!!! So full of mystery and excitement and treasures! If only we will take the time to search for Him beneath the surface by looking intently into His word. He longs for us to know Him...to trust Him...to be healed by His love.

We cannot wait to share the excitement of our trip to Duke! We are expecting to see our huge God do huge things this week! As someone recently reminded me...if we fail to ask God to do big things, it may be because we do not believe He is all that big and powerful of a God. Well...He is! So ask BIG!!!!

I am praying that you experience the BIGness of God this week! He's crazy about you!!!!

## *Day 1 at Duke...*

We met this morning with Victoria, a physician's assistant, and with Dr. Henry Friedman from the Duke Brain Tumor Center. We had a great visit and Mike has decided to enroll in the clinical trial that will enable him to receive Avastin. We will meet with more clinicians tomorrow to discuss details about treatment, schedules, insurance, etc., and then Mike is also going to have a full spine MRI at 1:00pm. We are planning to head back to Knoxville after that.

The day went pretty much as we had hoped. Mike prayed this morning that we would get to see Dr. Friedman (not always the case). No surprise...we did!!! Dr. Friedman said the surgery was very successful and that Mike was a good candidate for the study. Our time with him was brief; however, he did have time to slam UT basketball and conceded in admitting that the Lady Vols have a good program. He's a funny guy!!!!

Mike will most likely begin treatment at Thompson Cancer Center next week. We will come back to Duke in about 2 months. Praising God for this day!!!!!

## *Day 2 at Duke...*

It has been a good but long day! We met this morning with a nurse who went over the clinical trial protocol with a fine toothed comb. She was WONDERFUL and "dumbed" everything down so eloquently. She was fabulous and such a sweet lady! We feel even more confident about our decision after speaking with her. We also spoke with a host of other personnel who were incredibly helpful.

Next, Mike went to have his MRI (it is now 2pm) and then we headed back to the brain tumor center at 4pm and met with our clinical trial coordinator. She will keep us on track and communicate with Thompson Cancer Center. She is actually already working with Dr. McCachren who has another patient in this same study! We are so thankful to know she is there to make sure we know exactly what to do and when to do it, otherwise, our heads would be swimming! This all seems extremely complicated and overwhelming to us, but they talk as if it is all a walk in the park...as it should be for them! We did not get all our meetings in so we are going back in the morning for another short appointment with a licensed clinical social worker who will talk to us

53

about insurance and a few other details. She gave us the option to go home and follow up by phone, but we chose to stay and meet face-to-face with her so we don't leave feeling like we have loose ends to tie up. We want to leave here with a big sigh of relief and feeling as if we are completely prepared to start the battle that lies ahead.

God continues to completely infuse our hearts and minds with His peace. I was reading one of my favorite books with writings by Amy Carmichael[5] today while waiting on Mike to have his MRI done.  She wrote about the blessing we have (as God's children) to know and experience His power in our own lives. She reflected on Mark 4:39 - *"He got up, rebuked the wind and said to the waves, "Quiet! **Be still!**" Then the wind died down and it was completely calm."* That is exactly what Jesus has done in our lives these past few weeks. Jesus was not on a boat sleeping...He was calmly dwelling in our hearts, and when this storm hit we clung to Him in faith, believing that He had all the power needed to rebuke this storm! The waves are calm now and we are sailing this uncharted territory with peace and confidence that Jesus charts our course. Even the winds and waves obey Him...even this cancer obeys Him! He is sovereign over all! He speaks and it happens!

We have not reached the shore yet, and the wind and waves might rise up again, but we will sleep peacefully with Jesus trusting that we won't be tossed overboard! And eventually, the boat will reach the other side!

Praying that you will invite God's power to be unleashed in your life and that Jesus will bless you with a calmness of heart! Please know that our love and prayers go out to each of you as we journey together!

Floating along...

## *Quick update and prayer requests...*

We are SO glad to be home and under one roof with our kids! We came home feeling like everything is in place and that there are no loose ends to tie up! That was our prayer! Praise God for His grace and mercy and goodness! We also have great confidence that the Duke team and Thompson are on the ball and that is relieving much stress! Dr. McCachren actually has a patient who is participating in the same clinical trial that Mike will be in, so he and his staff are already familiar and comfortable with the protocol and our research coordinator. Go God!

What a blessing it is for us to be able to approach God's throne with confidence! We are so blessed to live on this side of the cross! There is nothing to keep us from entering into His presence...no barrier...no curtain...no rituals! Just free access to the very throne room where our Creator and Savior sit waiting to welcome us and hear our pleas! Can we really comprehend what a gift that is? WOW!

We are praying that you all have a blessed weekend. To those of you who fought to secure the freedoms we have today...THANK YOU! To all you service men, women, and families currently serving...THANK YOU! What a selfless sacrifice you make/made! THANK YOU!!!!! Happy Memorial Day!

Overwhelmed by it all...

## *Update on treatment schedule...*

Well...due to all the technical preparations, Mike will be starting treatments a bit later than we had thought. The radiation therapist at Thompson has been carefully programming the administration of radiation in order to make sure they avoid damaging vital neuro-cognitive functioning...we definitely don't want to speed that up! There was also a delay in receiving his chemo prescription. Mike will go back Friday morning for another scan to make sure all the radiation programming is accurate, and then he will have his first treatment on Monday, June 7 at 10:40 am. He will do radiation Monday through Friday for 6 weeks. Treatments are set up to take place every day at the same time - 10:40am. It is nice to finally have a start date and game plan. We are so thankful for the patient, conscientious staff at

Thompson who have worked so hard to help us!

*"But you, O LORD, are a shield around [us]; you are [our] glory, the one who holds [our] head[s] high."* Psalm 3:3 NLT

He, and He alone, is our strength and our hope. He lifts our heads and our downcast spirits when things become overwhelming, frustrating, confusing, and down right depressing! He is our LORD, Jehovah, our covenant keeping God who makes good on every promise He's made...promises we don't deserve, but still He graciously and mercifully gives! Every bit of this journey is sifted through His sovereign hands. We believe that! We accept that, and THAT is what sustains us and strengthens us! God IS good! Pressing on...

## The Big Day...

Tomorrow is the big day! Mike will begin taking his chemo drug and have his first radiation treatment. He will take his chemo pill at 9:40am and radiation is at 10:40. He will take Zofran as well to help prevent nausea. Please pray for the treatments to be tolerated and NO NAUSEA!!!! We have had a wonderful weekend and are going into the week well rested and ready to fight! Our God reigns!

*"I will go before you and will level the mountains; I will break down gates of bronze and cut through bars of iron. I will give you the treasures of darkness, riches stored in secret places, so that you may know that I am the LORD, the God of Israel, who summons you by name."* Isaiah 45:2-3

I am not sure if I am interpreting these verses correctly, or if I am using them out of context, but they speak to me in this circumstance and capture what we have found to be true this past month...there are some treasures of God that can only be found as we walk in the darkness of the valley. Like venturing deep into a cave where priceless gems or gold are hidden...God has treasures hidden away that can only be found when our fears and trials lead us deeper into His heart...the greatest treasure trove of all! Unfortunately, we cannot realize the beauty of these treasures compared to what we already have unless we actually find them...and then, we realize that what we once thought was our greatest treasure pales in comparison to what we find in these dark places.

When darkness comes, do not fear...trust that God will lead you to treasures untold...treasures tucked away in His heart which is full of love for you!

Tucked away...

# *Your Story...*

Throughout the Old Testament, God's people would erect monuments as reminders of what they had seen the Lord do on their behalf...physical, tangible reminders of His faithfulness in keeping His promises. Pause here and take some time to record some of the ways you have seen God working in your life...either recently or in the past...ways He has show himself faithful and sovereign in your life. There is nothing more powerful in terms of building our faith than recounting the many ways God has been faithful to keep His promises and actively work in our lives. Build yourself a monument to look back to in those moments when your faith is waning...it's O.K....we are all human and we all need those reminders!

Chapter Five

# Let The Games Begin...

"For I know the plans I have for you," declares the LORD, "plans to prosper you and not to harm you, plans to give you hope and a future."
*Jeremiah 29:11*

We really did not know what to expect regarding this leg of the journey. At this point, to be honest, our heads were still swimming with information. It felt great to have the Duke trip behind us. We felt confident in the treatment plan and hopeful that Mike would have a great chance to slay this giant. We headed into the treatment process with stones of Truth in our "slingshot" and ready to do battle...knowing without a doubt that God was fighting this battle for us...we just had to trust and pull the stones our of our pocket!

Despite the peace we felt in our hearts, there were still questions swirling around in our mind...*would Mike experience a lot of side effects from the chemo and radiation...would his hair fall out...how would the kids react to the side effects...what exactly was life going to look like?* As you might suspect, many of the answers to these questions did not come right away. We just had to sit back and "enjoy" the ride.

Friends and family, once again, surrounded us and absorbed much of the stress. Meals were delivered, rides to radiation were given, and prayers were offered on our behalf. Selfless servants came to our aid again and again. The love we received was almost overwhelming (in a good way). How could others love so selflessly? I have to admit that I struggled to feel worthy of such love. I often wrestled with guilt, asking myself if I show the same type of love to others in need. This part of the journey opened my eyes to a whole new dimension of God's love for me. Each time someone served us we saw Jesus in their smile...felt God's embrace in their hugs...heard God's voice in their words of encouragement and concern. We (Christians) are truly the body of Christ, used by God to reveal himself to others and to touch the hearts He formed. I hope and pray I will be able to pay all of this forward and further His kingdom and strengthen His church. As God's children, His grace is not only for us, it is for us to also give and share with others. Heaven forbid we should be stingy enough to keep it to ourselves!

The following journal entries in this chapter provide a glimpse into the 6 weeks Mike endured while taking his first round of chemo and radiation treatments.

# And we're off...

We just got home from radiation treatment number 1. I think it was a strange, surreal moment for Mike this morning as he swallowed his first chemo pill. Nonetheless...this leg of the journey has begun. So far, so good. Mike is feeling a little tired, but that may be from the anti-nausea medication, or it could be that all the built up adrenaline from anticipating this day has begun leaving his body. Regardless...I think he'll be catchin' a little nappy-poo this afternoon! Thanks for your prayers. We will keep you posted!

# So far, so good!

One more radiation treatment tomorrow and Mike will have finished week one! YAY!!! He has done amazingly well! Beyond our wildest dreams well! No nausea, just a little tired and that may not even be due to the medications or radiation! We are hopeful that the side effects will be minimal, but we are not foolish enough to think that it may not get any worse than this. His first Avastin treatment went great, too. It took about two hours and will gradually get shorter...down to about 30 minutes. They administer the same amount of drug; however, they administer it over a longer period of time at first in case he has an adverse reaction. He did not feel a thing today. Thank you all for praying. We KNOW it is making a difference! He is feeling great so far, so let's keep those prayers going, and let's all _praise God_ together for His wonderful mercy, grace,and goodness!!!!

Isn't it just so exciting to see God at work! He is such a powerful, huge God that cannot be defined by our finite minds...and that is OK because I don't want to worship a God whose power, wisdom, and might can be explained by mere words or human understanding. I want to worship a God who parts seas, makes time stand still, raises the dead, makes the blind see, casts out demons, changes lives, and loves with an everlasting love. It blows my mind that He is so intent on loving us and having a relationship with us. Makes me think of Psalm 8:3-4

*"I look up at your macro-skies, dark and enormous, your handmade sky-jewelry, Moon and stars mounted in their settings. Then I look at my micro-self and wonder, Why do you bother with us? Why take a second look our way?" The Message*

We are His prized creation and He loves us beyond what our finite minds can understand...even when we are blown away by His faithful, relentless love, we still have only scratched the surface of the depth of love that fills His heart. If only we knew...really knew How deep and perfect His love is! If we did, I think our lives would look a lot different, and I pray from here on that mine does!!!

Soaking up His love...

## *Week Three...Here We Come!!!*

Week two went super good. Although Mike started off the week feeling kind of cruddy, things got better as the week went on. We are thinking some of that was the effects of the first Avastin treatment last Thursday or possibly coming completely off the steroid....regardless, God answered many prayers this past week and we rejoice with praise and thanksgiving for His mercy! Mike's blood pressure and white/red blood cell counts were all good on Thursday.

As we head into week three, we have been advised to be prepared for a few things to develop...tenderness on his scalp and hair loss in the area that the radiation is being directed. The fatigue will most likely increase as well. Mike also has another Avastin dose on Thursday.

*"He is the Rock, his works are perfect, and all his ways are just. A faithful God who does no wrong, upright and just is he." Deut 32:4*

Thank you, Lord that You know our every need and that we can trust You to answer these prayers according to Your perfect will. We are here to glorify You...YOU are God...WE are Your creation...WE are here FOR YOU...may Your will be done! May our lives sing songs of praise to You...our Rock and our Redeemer! "Blessed be Your name when the sun's shinning down on us...when the world's all as it should be...blessed be Your name. Blessed be Your name on the road marked with suffering...when there's pain in the offering...blessed be Your name. Blessed be Your name when we walk in the wilderness...when we're found in the desert place...blessed be Your name!"[7] BLESSED BE YOUR NAME, LORD!!!! With every breath...we say...BLESSED BE YOUR NAME...YOU are so worthy of our praise and we love You!!!!

## *Even Though...*

Even though our spirits are crushed at times...we will still praise You, Lord! Even though the darkness surrounds us at times...we will still praise You, Lord! Even though our circumstances scare us at times...we will still praise You, Lord! Even though our hearts are sometimes filled with grief and frustration...we will still praise You, Lord! Even though we are completely helpless to change this...we will still praise You, Lord! Even though we cannot make sense of this...we will still praise You, Lord!

We will praise You, Lord, because Your unfailing love sustains us and comforts us through this storm. We will praise You, Lord, because You have proven Your faithfulness and love for us by sending Your Son. We will praise You, Lord, because You deserve our praise! We will praise You, Lord, because we know that You hold our future in Your hands. We will praise You, Lord, because You have filled our hearts with a hope and joy that cannot be stolen or destroyed by anything in this world when we choose to believe and receive. We have gazed upon You and seen Your glory and strength - we will praise You, Lord because Your love IS better than life...so we will praise You as long as we live. You have done great things for us, Lord, and we are filled with joy (Ps 126:3)!

Well...Mike has made it through week three. This coming Tuesday, he will have surpassed the half way mark of phase I of his treatment plan (33 days of radiation, chemo, and Avastin). For the most part, the week went well. His scalp continues to become more sensitive and he is losing most of the hair on the left side of his head/face. He is also feeling pretty fatigued. He had an Avastin treatment on Thursday, and that really took the wind out of his sails. He had a rough day Saturday and felt REALLY cruddy. Today, however, he has regained some strength and was able to enjoy Mallory's birthday party.

We anticipate that the effects of the radiation and Avastin will build in the days ahead. From what we've been told, the second half of treatment feels like a marathon, so to speak. Our focus is for Mike to have enough stamina to make it through each day, rather than enough stamina to make it through the end of treatment. The former seems much more manageable.

Mike's spirits are good! I have to admit that I am having a difficult time watching him suffer. It was hard being at church without him this morning. Nevertheless...as we continue to tuck ourselves into God, we are strengthened, comforted, and encouraged! He is for us, and He WILL NOT FAIL US!

Thank you all for loving us and for encouraging us. Your notes of encouragement always seem to come at just the right time with just the right words! We feel like the Lord has used you all to surround us and protect us from the doubt, deception, and discouragement that is always lurking about! It seems to take a lot of energy just to win the battle in our minds and take our thoughts captive. We are putting on our armor and swinging the sword of truth at whatever Satan tries to throw our way! There is much to be learned on this journey, and we do not want to miss what God has in store for us to take hold of.

Well...I've officially progressed to rambling, so I am going to wrap this up. Praying that you all will gaze upon His glory and strength this week and that your hearts will truly proclaim...His love is better than life!

Praising Him...even though...

## Singing His Praises...

Today is Wednesday...Mike is feeling MUCH better!!!! Praise the Lord! I read this quote today in *Streams In The Desert*[7]..."Nothing lies beyond the reach of prayer except those things outside the will of God." We know that when we pray in Jesus name, seeking God's perfect will, our prayers WILL be answered! John 14:13-14 says...*"And I will do whatever you ask in my name, so that the Father may be glorified in the Son. You may ask me for anything in my name, and I will do it."* There it is...straight from God's Word! In His name, seeking His will, and desiring that He be glorified...we lift our prayers...and He is answering!

In case you can't "hear" the excitement and praise in my written words, just use your imagination!!!! We are rejoicing and we know you are too.

Singing His praises...

## WEEK 5 ?!?!?!?!?!

WOW...are we really starting week 5? Well...I guess we are! Only 13 more radiation treatments. Time flies when you are being radiated! Mike had a pretty good week. He continues to have mild nausea and fatigue, but he is still able to take walks in the morning, his appetite is good, and he is sleeping well. God is certainly showing this cancer who's boss and He is reminding the enemy that He and He alone is sovereign and crazy in love with His children!

Please remember to pray for Mike this week...it is Avastin week. His blood pressure was creeping up a bit at the end of last week...not bad, just a bit. Please pray that it will stay down as this is the main side effect of the Avastin. A very high percentage (like 75% I think) of people taking Avastin end up on blood pressure meds. Pray that Mike won't need them! His blood counts continue to be excellent! Huge praise!

God continues to WOW us daily! We hope and pray that these updates are allowing you to be WOW-ed by God, too! We give Him all the credit for Mike's progress and health. Hope you all enjoyed your 4th of July weekend. We had a great time enjoying friends and shooting off fireworks in the neighborhood...although we almost got blown up! I guess that is about it. I look forward to posting more good news later this week.

## The Countdown...

Today is a big day! The number of radiation treatments left has entered SINGLE DIGITS...woohoo!!!! That calls for a celebration. Stop right now and do a happy dance. Seriously...go ahead...bust a move! So far, Mike is doing well. He is a bit more fatigued and felt pretty cruddy last night, but he is doing well after Avastin treatment 3. His blood pressure and blood counts were good this week! Praise the Lord!

From the get-go, Isaiah 42:16 has been a verse that has brought us much comfort and courage. God continues to lead us down this unfamiliar path, and at times, we have certainly felt "blind". He has turned darkness into light as He has walked before us making the rough places smooth and easier to travel. Knowing and believing His promises has allowed us to endure and not fall into the pits of fear that line this path. The fires have been hot and at times we have felt scorched, but He is a faithful firewall. The waters have been rough and at times we have feared going under, but He has been our life vest. This path stinks, but He has never left or forsaken us...it is the path He has chosen, therefore, He will light each step and protect us as the fires refine us.

Still dancing...

# *A Peek Into Heaven...*

I was thinking the other day about just how amazing it would be to peek into the heavenly realm. What does God look like and sound like when He sings over us (Zeph. 3:17)? Does the Holy Spirit kneel when He intercedes for me or does He just have a sit down with the Father (Romans 8:26)? Is the sound of all the creatures surrounding His throne crying "holy, holy, holy" deafening (Rev 4:8)?

As I pondered these thoughts this morning, God spoke back and this is what He said..."Every time you receive an encouraging note in the mail or have someone stop you and share words of encouragement, you have heard and seen Me sing over you. When you see others kneeling or bowing in prayer, or when you have held the hands of a friend while they prayed for you, your eyes have seen the Holy Spirit interceding on your behalf. When you see or hear the heart of My children proclaiming My glory and wonder, you have caught a glimpse of the praises going on in heaven which are the sweetest sounds you will ever hear."

Because of Jesus, we can approach God's throne of grace with confidence and enter into the holy of holies (Hebrews 10:19). God's Spirit in us allows us to see and know things beyond what our human, finite minds and eyes can see and comprehend (1 Cor. 2:10). When we live as God desires us to live, and love on another as God desires us to love, we see glimpses of Him...glimpses of heaven on earth.

Thank you all for loving us...for opening up heaven for us...for carrying us to the throne and into the holy of holies. I don't know if we can ever truly experience the pureness of heaven here on earth, but this has to be about as close as we could ever get...and each of you...your words and acts of love...have been the evidence of things unseen by our human eyes...glimpses into heaven and glimpses of the pure and beautiful glory of God and His perfectly pure love!

Thank you just doesn't cut it, but we are asking the Father to speak to your hearts and translate our words so that you will comprehend the hugeness of our gratitude. Our deepest prayer is that you will also see His glory and feel His touch as you journey with us. He is a God who relentlessly pursues us out of a deep desire and determination to love us and bless us. Don't miss it...don't miss all that He has in store... *"...'No eye has seen, no ear has heard, and no mind has imagined what God has prepared for those who love him.' But it was to us that God revealed these things by his Spirit. For his Spirit searches out everything and shows us God's deep secrets. No one can know a person's thoughts except that person's own spirit, and no one can know God's thoughts except God's own Spirit. And we have received God's Spirit (not the world's spirit), so we can know the wonderful things God has freely given us."* (I Cor. 2:9-13 NLT). He does not want us to miss it and He has sacrificed so much in order that we might receive all that He has in store!

In awe of what I've seen...

## *Winding Down...*

Phase one of treatment is winding down this week. Only 4 radiation treatments and one Avastin treatment left. Mike takes his last chemo pill in the morning. It is hard to believe how fast the past 6 weeks have flown by, and at the same time it has been the longest 6 weeks of our life. Mike is looking forward to his almost three week break before heading back to Duke and beginning phase 2 of the clinical trial.

This has been the roughest week by far. Mike has felt more fatigue, more nausea, and just generally more cruddy. It is pretty sad that "cruddy" has become a common word in our daily vocabulary! Nevertheless, I am amazed by Mike's strength and self-discipline...AMAZED!!!! He is still getting up every morning and walking 2 miles...whether he feels like it or not. Thursday morning he got back from his walk and said it felt like he had walked through knee deep mud. Friday morning was better. He had a pretty good day today and then all of the sudden this evening he went downhill and felt terrible. There does not really seem to be a pattern to how he feels which is frustrating.

His appetite is not as good and foods that he once loved are now difficult to eat...they just don't taste the same.

When he had his blood work done this Thursday, his platelets had dipped down a bit so pray that this is not a trend that will continue. White and red blood cell counts were still good and blood pressure was OK as well. We are hoping that since he is finishing chemo tomorrow that his blood counts will stay up and that he will rebound a bit during the next three weeks.

Let's all pray the heavens down this week and help Mike get through this final leg of radiation. Pray that the machines stay up and running. Pray that Mike's stamina will improve. Pray that his spirits will be uplifted. Pray that he will look forward to spending some time at the lake in Indiana with his family. Pray that he will be able to celebrate this phase coming to an end and not focus on the remainder of treatments and the mountain he still has to climb.

"The journey is arduous at times, and you are weak. Someday you will dance light-footed on the high peaks; but for now, your walk is often plodding and heavy. All I require of you is to take the next step, clinging to My hand for strength and direction. Though the path is difficult and the scenery dull at the moment, there are sparkling surprises just around the bend. Stay on the path I have selected for you. It is truly the path of life."[8]. Those words speak volumes to my heart today! Thank you, Jesus for calling me to your side...for leading me to your heart!

*"A man's steps are established by the LORD, and He takes pleasure in his way. Though he falls, he will not be overwhelmed, because the LORD holds his hand"* Psalm 37:23-24 HCSB

It is impossible to go through this journey without clinging to His promises. What a blessing that we have them in writing and that we can go to them at any moment and find the peace our hearts are longing for...regardless of the circumstance. The moment I open His Word and begin to treasure His promises, my heart is calm and His perfect love cast out all my fears and anxiety. He leads me beside still waters!

He IS the Good Shepherd!

## More Than <u>WE</u> Can Handle...

I had some time today to just sit and think about the many lessons God has taught me over the past couple of months. His Truth has shined so much brighter as we have walked so closely with Him on this journey. There just seems to be a new depth and richness to His Word. Not that it was not important to us before, but it just seems that a layer of fuzz or a cloud of mist has been blown away by His love, revealing truths to us more vividly. It is difficult to accurately describe what I am trying to communicate, but maybe you can relate.

I am sure I have said this hundreds of times as I have tried to encourage or console someone, and maybe you have too, but I now realize that my words were misleading..."God will not give you more than you can handle." I now realize that this could not be farther from the truth. Why do we say such a thing? To make someone feel better I suppose. The truth is, God will certainly give us more than WE can handle; however, He will NEVER give us more than HE can handle. In an effort to teach us to more fully rely on Him, God will most definitely allow circumstances to come into our lives that leave us helpless and in need of His sovereign strength. His strength is made perfect in our weakness and His grace is completely sufficient for our every need (II Cor. 12:9). He will never leave us or forsake us (Deut. 31:8). We can cast all our cares upon Him and know that He will carry the weight of our burdens (I Peter 5:7). And, when we are at our weakest and in our most weary moments...relying on His strength...placing our hope in Him... and surrendering all our needs to Him...He will lift us up and allow our spirits to soar high and free above our circumstances (Isaiah 40:31).

Why do we work so hard trying to avoid and prevent the very circumstances that can bring us closest to the heart of God...pain,

70

suffering, loss, helplessness...it is in these moments that we are able to experience the true power of God's grace. It is also in these moments that we are able to realize just how often we settle for relying on our own strength. It is so freeing to recognize the difference. It is through suffering and intimate fellowship with Christ that we begin to understand and experience the awesomeness of His resurrection power. Paul said it best...*"I gave up all that inferior stuff so I could know Christ personally, experience his resurrection power, be a partner in his suffering, and go all the way with him to death itself. If there was any way to get in on the resurrection from the dead, I wanted to do it."* Phil 3:10 The Message

Our "determined purpose" throughout this journey has been that we might know Him more and that we might be transformed as a result of our "suffering". God has been so faithful to answer our prayers and to reveal Himself to us like never before. My hope and prayer is that you, too, will experience Christ more intimately each and every day...that you will have a determined purpose to seek Him and know Him and live for Him. God is calling us to share His love with a broken world...to share HIM with a broken world so that they might find healing and the hope that their hearts are longing for.

Thank you for allowing me to ramble and share my heart. These journal entries have been so therapeutic for me! Moments when I can express my heart and show my gratitude to God for how incredibly gracious and faithful He has been to my family.

Mike just has two radiation treatments left. Woohoo!!!!!! I can hardly believe it! He is tired and ready for a break, but his spirit is strong! I am so proud of him and so thankful that God gave me such an incredible husband. I don't deserve him, but I sure am glad he's mine! Love you honey!

Soaring on His wings...

71

## Graduation Celebration...

He made it! Thursday was the last radiation and last Avastin for a few weeks. One of the radiation techs, who is a dear friend of ours, told us that she cannot remember when a patient has sailed through radiation as easily as Mike did. The machine never went down and he did not miss one single day (except for the 4th holiday). I'm guessing most of the other patients don't have thousands of people praying all over the world...but I hope they do!!!!! So remember to pray for them when you pray for Mike.

We left for Indiana right after Mike's treatment and got here around 11:30 last night. We've enjoyed our first day at the lake. Mike is feeling pretty tired...he took a big nap this afternoon and now he is feeling a bit better. We are looking forward to some much needed R&R and this is the perfect place to do that!

Catching our breath...bracing for the next storm!

# Your Story...

Do you ever find it difficult to believe...really believe...that God "knows the plans He has for you" and that these plans are for your good and not to harm you? Are you going through a crisis right now that might cause you to doubt God's promise in Jeremiah 29:11? Chances are, you can (or could have in the past) answer "yes" to these questions. How might Jeremiah 29:11 and Romans 8:28 work together to encourage you right now? Look up these verses and spend some time talking to God about what you (or someone you know) are going through. Do you need God to increase your faith? Do you need to accept your circumstances and trust that God does have a plan in all this...a plan that is for your good, not to harm you? These are questions that we must all consider and answer when going through a crisis. Spend some honest time with the Lord...

Chapter Six

# A Little R and R

*"He will cover you with His feathers; you will take refuge under His wings. His faithfulness will be a protective shield." Psalm 91:4 HCSB*

Within hours after Mike finished he last radiation and Avastin treatment, we hit the road for Indiana.  His mom and dad live on a small lake in northern Indiana and we look forward to visiting every summer, but this summer, we were exceedingly grateful to have such a wonderful, peaceful place to retreat to and rest in the stillness and beautiful scenery God has created.

The first round of treatment (chemo, radiation, and Avastin) took a toll on Mike's body. He was tired, weak, bald, and slightly crispy. I am not even sure if crispy is the best choice of words. In fact, I am not sure what adjective best describes the condition of the skin on his forehead and scalp.  He had to wear a mask during radiation that was bolted down to the radiation table in order to keep his head perfectly still.  The mask was made up of a very stiff mesh material that resembles a fish net.  As a result, he was left with a lovely "fish net" motif covering his face from his eyebrows up.  It was as if he got a sun tan while laying in the sun with a fishnet over his face.  I am sure that this conjures up quite an image in your imagination.  If you are thinking *Wow! How strange*...you are spot on. It was a bit strange looking, but he is as handsome as ever!  He was also completely bald except for a small patch of hair on the back of his head where he rested on a cushion while laying on the radiation table.  In case you are wondering...yes...men can be vain.  I think this new look was a bit uncomfortable for Mike, but I assured him it looks great...*considering*!!!

So...there we were...in a beautiful place to relax...no running back and forth to the cancer treatment center every day...just a cool breeze and some soft, green grass...oh, and a pack of sunflower seeds to help pass the time.  Aaaahhhh!  I am relaxing just thinking about how wonderful it was!

## *Resting...*

We are having such a wonderful time at the lake visiting Mike's parents! It is just so beautiful and peaceful here...lots of time to be still...reflect...soak...and just plain relax! I think we are all breathing a huge sigh of relief! The first few days were rough for Mike. He was exhausted and felt like he had been run over by a steamroller. By Tuesday, he was feeling MUCH better and we even went kayaking around the lake (that's right Kent and Amy...we went kayaking). Wednesday afternoon, Mike and I drove up to Shipshewana...an Amish town about an hour north...and saw a play titled <u>The Rock, The Redeemer, and the Resurrection Morning</u>. It was wonderful...we laughed and celebrated the goodness and wonderfulness of God...great story and incredible music. Today, Mike went kayaking with his mom and went out on the lake in the boat while the kids went tubing. I don't think he has even taken a nap today. Oh...Mike has also been walking three miles every morning. Even on the days that he felt so terrible...he was out walking. That's Mike for ya!!!!

One of the things I enjoy most about coming to the lake each summer is the solitude and serenity I get to enjoy. This year, everything seems to be in HD...birds sing louder, flowers are more vivid, the air smells sweeter...and, best of all, God's voice is louder and clearer! Satan has been tempting me to believe the lie that the peace and joy I have in the midst of this storm are merely my strong defense mechanisms kicking in to protect me from the pain and reality of what is going on. However, God and I have had some long talks this week and He has assured me that I am experiencing exactly what He promises to those who place their trust in Him and those who abide in Him. John 15 and Romans 8 have reminded me of these truths. Our victory over these circumstances is not defined/measured by the outcome of the circumstance but by our ability to trust God completely! Our ultimate victory has already been won. Colossians 2:15 tells us that! Thankfully, Romans 8 encourages us and reminds us that we can be MORE than victorious...our ultimate victory is in heaven...but we can also celebrate our victory even in the midst of trials because NOTHING can separate us from the love of Christ! This peace and joy that I feel in my heart, even in the midst of such pain and confusion, is MOST CERTAINLY REAL! So...Satan can just stick that in his pipe and smoke it!

Trusting God's heart completely, I know that He has a plan and a purpose for this. I don't know why His will for Mike involves allowing him to have cancer, but it does. If that is the case, then He will also provide every ounce of grace we need to accomplish the good work He began in us. This is true of each and every one of us! God is longing for us all to know...TRULY KNOW...how deep and high and wide His love is. He longs for us to be so completely full of His joy and peace that our lives overflow with a message of hope to all we come in contact with. He is such a faithful God and I thank Him for correcting my spiritual vision so that I can see Him more clearly and so that I can see truth more clearly. Our vision is often clouded by pride, fear, lust, greed, pain...the list goes on. In order to have 20/20 spiritual vision, we must look at everything through His eyes. That can be a challenge, but He is faithful and He will always shine His light into our darkness/blurred vision if we earnestly seek Him. Ahhhhh...I just had to get that off my chest.

Enjoying the stillness...

## *It Is Not Good For Man To Be Alone...*

I left Indiana before Mike and the kids in order to come home and get ready to start my new job. I am soooo excited that my family is coming home tomorrow. I miss them terribly! I went to bed last night with a massive headache and it was still there this morning...ugh! I don't even remember turning off the alarm this morning (which was suppose to get me up in time for an activity at church...oooops!). Nevertheless...I have projects to get done before everyone gets back, so I had to suck it up. Most importantly, I needed to make room to put Mike's car back in the garage before he gets home...lol! Long story, but I brought home a few "treasures" that I found in the family barn and Mike insisted that he not come home to find his side of the garage filled and taking up his space.

So...as I was cleaning up my barn treasures in the garage, I decided to multitask and have a talk with the Lord. For some reason, our conversation turned toward how it was for me to be alone this past week. He spoke to me about how vulnerable we are when we do not have others there to help us...to confide in...to hold us accountable. Left alone, the enemy recognizes our vulnerability and temps us with his sly voice of deception. I thought about Eve in the garden when she was ALONE and tempted by the serpent. I thought about how God said...it is not good for man to be alone. I thought about how, in the New Testament, believers are reminded again and again to gather together, to lean on one another, to encourage one another, to hold each other accountable. Ok...I just thought about how this might sound...me alone last week and God talking to me about temptation... rest assured...there is nothing more to this other than God showing me just how amazingly blessed I am to have so many wonderful believers surrounding me, loving me, and praying for me.

In our current situation, I have learned how important it is to have others who will comfort me, encourage me, pray for me, and help me. What a beautiful picture of the body of Christ...the church...displaying the love of Christ and mission of Christ. I think God is teaching me just how vital it is to get my eyes off myself and to remember that one of my most important purposes in this life is to love my neighbor as myself...to care for my "neighbor's" needs above my own...to care about my "neighbor's" hurts...to recognize how God might choose to meet my "neighbor's" needs through me. God has taught me so much by the faithfulness of others to do this in my family's life.

It is not good for man to be alone...what a blessing it is that God is with us and that we have one another to "be" Jesus' hands and feet and arms of love in our life when we need to feel His touch...literally! I enjoyed my talk with the Lord today, and...my headache is much better, and...I can fit Mike's car back in the garage, and...my family is coming home tomorrow! It's been a good day! Never alone...

# Back To Duke...

Pray...Pray...Pray...and Pray some more!!!! We just got to the hotel in Durham. Mike will have an MRI tomorrow at 10:00am and then we will meet with the doctor at the brain tumor center at 12:00pm. We should have the results of the MRI when we meet with the doctor. Please pray with us for a CLEAN MRI! We are so thankful for the peace that God has poured into our hearts. As we drove this afternoon and evening, we talked about many of the ways we have seen God's providence and sovereignty displayed in the details of our lives with respect to our current situation. Even going back as far as a year a go, we see how His hand orchestrated so many details that have prepared us for this journey and given us confidence that He has been in control and is providing our every need each step of the way...even when we have not been aware...we CAN look back and see His fingerprints! He is such a gracious Father!

Again, I am resting in Psalm 116:1-2 *"I love the Lord because he hears my voice and my prayer for mercy. Because he bends down to listen, I will pray as long as I have breath!" (NLT)* I sure would love to see what that looks like...the King of all creation bending down to hear my measly voice and my pitiful prayers! I bet He is smiling when He does it! I bet there is mercy and tenderness in His eyes. After all, He rejoices over me (and you) with singing. I cannot wait to post the next update...I am counting on it being a celebration of the miraculous!

Praying without ceasing...

# Go God!!!!!

Whew...as you can imagine, we are soooo relieved to have gotten the news we got at Duke yesterday. The physician's assistant said Mike's MRI was "beautiful". She was amazed and so excited by just how good it looked. After our bodies had completely deflated from a huge

78

sigh of relief, we began celebrating and praising God. We have no doubt that Mike's progress and tolerance of treatment thus far are direct results of and answers to the thousands of prayers lifted up on our behalf and evidence of God's amazing grace and mercy. For some reason, I couldn't help but think about Joshua leading his men in battle and God hurling hailstones down from heaven. With sovereign precision, God struck down more of Israel's enemy, the Amorites, by these hailstones than by the swords of the Israelites (Joshua 10:11). God's sovereignty and providence trump any and every human power. I have always loved this story and pictured in my mind how amazing that must have been to be an eye-witness of God's awesome power! We are thankful for the wonderful doctors that are treating Mike and for modern medicine; however, we know that God is using them and directing them by His sovereignty to bring about His will according to His plan!!!!

We are so happy that Mike's MRI was clean, but the battle is not over yet! He begins phase two of treatment tomorrow assuming his medication arrives on time through the mail. Phase two consists of twelve 28 day cycles (so basically a year). During each 28 day cycle (i.e. month), he will take two types of chemo days 1-6 (oral) and have an Avastin treatment every other week (which is administered by IV). The chemo dosage is much stronger this round, but he only takes chemo a total of six days per month rather than every day as he did during radiation. The side effects should be similar to phase one. We are hoping that with radiation out of the mix, his fatigue will be less of an issue. The main concerns are blood count issues from the chemo and blood pressure issues from the Avastin.

We are so happy and content with the news we received yesterday. I wish we could say that we know what our future holds, but we don't. In reality, none of us does! We are just more keenly aware of that fact now! I know I have said this many times in my posts, but I will say it again...this journey has been a gift! As scary and frustrating as it is, I can honestly say "thank you" to God for allowing me to experience this new level of trust and faith in Him...for this new depth of dependence

79

on and surrender to Him...for this new understanding of my desperate need for Him. We are powerless to change our circumstances, but God has all the power we need to defeat every giant we will face...whether our need is for strength and faith or for complete healing...He promises to provide all our needs through His glorious riches in Christ, and through Him, we can do all things...even this! His banner over us is love and He IS our strong and mighty tower...our refuge and comfort...our friend and Father...our healer...our Savior...our strength...our all in all. He will not fail us!

Suddenly, the beauty of this world and all that we love in this world leaves us incredibly unsatisfied. Our eyes have been opened to see the eternal more clearly and we want more of Him and less of what this world has to offer...and He is so gracious to give! I am reminded of a passage of scripture that God opened my eyes and heart to not long after I had become a Christian. I was struggling with my willingness to stop living my old lifestyle and making a commitment to start living one that would bring glory and honor to Him. I wanted desperately to have both my feet fully and firmly planted in His will rather than "straddling the fence" so to speak. Through these words, God began to show me that nothing in this world will ever bring the satisfaction and peace my soul was longing for.

*"Come, all you who are thirsty,*
*come to the waters;*
*and you who have no money,*
*come, buy and eat!*
*Come, buy wine and milk*
*without money and without cost.*
*Why spend money on what is not bread,*
*and your labor on what does not satisfy?*
*Listen, listen to me, and eat what is good,*
*and your soul will delight in the richest of fare."*
Isaiah 55:1-2

Satisfied...

# *Your Story...*

Sometimes, when life gets hard, we run the risk of drifting further away from God rather than nearer to Him and His loving heart. For whatever reason, we tend to look to "the world" for the solutions to our problems rather than trusting in and abiding in (resting in) the promises and faithfulness of God. Take a few moments to think about whether or not you are abiding in (resting in) God's love. Have you run to Him and taken shelter in His loving care? Record your thoughts. Pause and pray for yourself or someone you know who is need of God's sheltering love.

Chapter Seven

# Buckling Up For A Bumpy Ride...

*"I raise my eyes toward the mountains. Where will my help come from? My help comes from the LORD, the Maker of heaven and earth. He will not allow your foot to slip; your Protector will not slumber. Indeed, the Protector of Israel does not slumber or sleep. The LORD protects you; the LORD is a shelter right by your side" Psalm 121:1-5 HCSB*

Over the past week, God has been so gracious to show me glimpses of His glory and tender love. Wednesday night, while I was blow drying Mallory's hair, she said, "Mom, I think I know why God allowed Dad to have cancer...so that others could see His power." Thursday, the first day of school, I saw Davis sitting at the lunch table laughing and talking with a group of boys...a simple yet sweet reminder that the Lord loves my children far more than I could ever dream of loving them. Friday afternoon, I saw some of Mallory's homework sitting on the kitchen table, and I picked it up to read, "My hero is my dad...he helps me when I am hurt...he fights hard against his cancer". Had I been in that hopeless cell of darkness...focused on the hugeness of my circumstances rather than the hugeness of God, I don't think I would have had eyes to see those little blessings. *"My eyes are ever on the LORD, for only he will release my feet from the snare."* Psalm 25:15

The choice is ours...what will we fix our eyes on when life is hard...even when life is good? Will we fix our eyes on Jesus, the author and perfector of our faith, or will we fix our eyes on ourselves and expect that God will only work in our lives through comfortable, desirable circumstances...if so, others' eyes would most likely be on us, not Him! They would admire us, not Him. They would praise us, not Him. They would seek to know us, not Him. They would seek our advice and wisdom, not His.

Lift up your eyes to the hills...where does your help come from...your help comes from the Lord- the maker of heaven and earth! (Psalm 121). His wonders never cease and He longs for us to see glimpses of His glory as we go about our days...evidence of His great love for us! He is with us and He is for us! What a mighty God we serve!

This chapter paints a vivid picture of what life is like when cancer treatment "gets rough." You might notice that the "tone" of these entries is a bit different. I would describe this leg of the journey as a reality check with respect to our recognition and acceptance of our "new normal." Yes...this part of the journey was tough, but it was also blessed! As we began to feel the sting of our pain more intensely, we also felt the miracle of God's grace more deeply, and we were even more in awe of His glory...

## *Perspective....*

Ugh...today has been one of those days that I have had to remind myself of a formula I have encouraged others to live by. Don't ya just love it when your own words come back to bite ya in the you know what (lol!). The formula is simple yet often difficult to follow. Circumstances + Perspective = Experience. I am reminded today that the only part of this equation that I can change is my perspective if I want to affect how I experience life. So...I am choosing to respond to life based on what I know to be true rather than responding based on my emotions. Responding to life based on my emotions today would have left me experiencing life curled up in my closet in the fetal position. But Truth has served me well!!!!! In my spirit, I feel as though I am standing proud atop a mountain with shield and sword in hand and my defeated foe under foot! But, I must admit, this battle has left me a bit bloody and bruised...and tired!

I am more than a conqueror through the power of my Savior who loves me...pressed but NOT CRUSHED...persecuted but NOT ABANDONED...struck down but NOT DESTROYED...I am blessed beyond the curse for His promises endure and HIS JOY is my strength!!!!!!

Please remember to pray for Mike. He had his first Avastin treatment on Monday. This evening he is feeling a bit tired and queasy. Pray for the kids as they continue to adjust to their new school. Pray for me to find time to be emptied of stress and filled with His Spirit.

Taking a deep Jesus breath...

# *When Love Involves Pain...*

Wow...it has been a rough week. It started off great...we hit a few bumps...things settled down...then another wave hit. I am exhausted! Mike is not tolerating this round of chemo very well. He did pretty good until Wednesday and then it hit him like a ton of bricks. He felt pretty bad on Thursday, but managed to make it through the day just feeling a little queasy. He came to pick the kids up from school Thursday afternoon and I could tell by looking at him, things were getting tough. By Friday, things were worse and Friday evening he ended up getting sick three times. The kids had a lock in Friday night. I picked them up Saturday morning around 7am. We came home and all went to bed. I woke up about 1:30 that afternoon and everyone was crashed in bed. Mike did not do much besides rotate between the bed and recliner. He is very quiet...probably because moving around and talking only magnifies the nausea. He did not sleep much last night. We are praying that since last night was his last dose of chemo for this cycle that he will begin feeling better in a few days! Please, Lord...let that be the case!

The most difficult thing for me these past few days has been watching Mike feel so miserable and not be able to do anything to help. You never know how much you love someone or how strong your love is until you have to go through some type of struggle together. I don't know about you, but my natural response to pain is to run from it...to make it go away. Well...I can neither run from this pain nor can I make it go away...I must simply endure it! These past few days, I have thought about what the Bible teaches us about covenant...a binding agreement between two people...so binding that the two become one. I thought about how Jesus took our sins and sorrow and made them His very own because of the covenant He has made with us. He took on our sin to the point of dying for us in order to demonstrate the depths of His love...the very basis of this covenant promise is to always be for us and with us. He humbled Himself and died for us even though He had every right to just leave and return to His throne.

I have never loved Mike more deeply than I love him now.
Maybe I have, but I definitely have not had to agonize and hurt for him
like I have the past week. My love for him has caused me a great deal of
pain lately. But, as we see from Jesus' example, sometimes love involves
pain. Two become one when they enter into a covenant...a binding
promise. I choose to endure the pain of watching Mike suffer because I
love him! I hurt because he hurts.

As a counselor, I've met with many couples who are having
problems in their marriages because they do not want to share the
burdens of their spouse or work through the challenges they face in
loving one another. When pain comes, for whatever reason, one spouse
chooses to walk away or neither spouse is willing to work through the
pain. Did they forget the promises they made..."for better or for
worse...in sickness and in health"...or did they just not consider the cost
of those words? When pain is the result of love, it CAN make love
stronger...IF one chooses to accept the pain and endure it for the sake of
love and honoring the covenant of marriage. I know that things can
always be "complicated", but "complicated" circumstances should never
trump or compromise truth, and the truth is... love should endure all
things! I know my circumstances are different from anyone else;
however, I felt the Lord impressing upon my heart to share these words.
I was hesitant to do so for fear that my words might be misunderstood
or taken the wrong way. I think the Lord was just helping me to see the
beauty of His enduring love and faithfulness which should be a model
for marriage. There is no room for selfishness in a marriage. When we
refuse to allow hardship to drive a wedge into our marriage, we in
essence allow God to use the circumstance to instead serve as a cord
that binds our hearts closer together.

I do not enjoy seeing Mike suffer! I am asking the Lord to give
me a tender heart towards him and to use the pain that I am feeling to
help me love him more deeply and to understand God's heart and love
for me more clearly. When love involves pain, there is a purpose...the
pain is like a rich fertilizer that makes love grow stronger and more
deeply rooted. If your love for someone involves pain (for whatever

reason) ask the Lord to give you whatever you need (strength, courage, perseverance, humility, etc.) to endure! Trust His faithfulness to use the pain to make your love stronger and the relationship more beautiful. He is faithful and He will do it! The change may only take place in you...or it may take place in the one you love...or both.

Enduring the pain...

## *No Matter What...*

There is a song being played on the radio these days that echo's the cry of my heart...no matter what...I'm gonna trust and love You Lord! You could so easily take this pain and trial away, but even if You don't...I will still trust You. I will run to Your promises and be lifted to a place of peace and joy! NO MATTER WHAT! I am so thankful for Christian music. God uses it time and time again to speak to and encourage my heart and transform my mind.

Today, I am running to these promises... *"I will praise you, O LORD, with all my heart; before the "gods" I will sing your praise. I will bow down toward your holy temple and will praise your name for your love and your faithfulness, for you have exalted above all things your name and your word. When I called, you answered me; you made me bold and stouthearted. Though I walk in the midst of trouble, you preserve my life; you stretch out your hand against the anger of my foes, with your right hand you save me. The LORD will fulfill his purpose for me; your love, O LORD, endures forever— do not abandon the works of your hands."* Psalm 138:1-3;7,8.

When we call, the Lord answers and makes us BOLD and STOUTHEARTED! He WILL fulfill His purpose for our lives...even if His purpose includes such a painful trial as this...we will believe and find strength in this promise. He is faithful...He will not abandon us...He stretches out His hand against our foe...cancer. This evil disease is limited by and submissive to the sovereign hand of God! My heart and

spirit are feeling exceptionally bold and stouthearted today!
Bursting with joy...

## Our New Normal...

We've had a wonderful weekend. Mallory and I left after school
on Friday and headed to Atlanta for a long awaited trip to the American
Girl store. She has been saving her money all year. We had such a great
time. Lots of laughs, snuggling in the king size bed, lots of eating, lots of
shopping...good quality time for mom and her girl! Mike and Davis were
actually able to go to the UT game Saturday. They had a great time as
well. We spent Sunday afternoon in the mountains with great
friends...very relaxing! It is moments like these that make life seem so
ordinary and "normal". And then there are the moments that hit me
square in the face and remind me of the stark reality...my husband has
cancer. Although so much in our daily lives has changed over the past 5
months, for the most part, it feels "normal" most of the time. But there
are those moments that sneak up on me and just about take my breath
away and make me physically nauseated. Like today when we were at
the grocery store. Mike went to get something we had forgotten while I
was in the checkout line. All of the sudden, I looked up and saw him
walking towards me and, wham, reality smacked me in the face. I was
looking at a man who looked very familiar, but at the same time, so
different. It is difficult to mesh these two worlds together sometimes.

Thank the Lord, I live mostly in the "everything is normal" world,
and the moments of reality don't seem to suck the life out of me for
long. I catch my breath and remind myself that God is in control and we
"can do this." With God, all things are possible...even this!

There is no time to be sucked into the pit of despair! What a
waste it would be to live life there. Instead, I choose to live in the here
and now, enjoying every moment and remembering that even when
Mike is getting on my nerves and the kids have worn me out...I love my
life and I am thankful for the blessing of each and every new day (inject
a tone of humor here!). God has blessed us beyond my wildest dreams.

As a friend recently reminded me...this is our new normal. To sit around and wait for our old life to return would be a huge waste of time...it is not going to happen. This IS our new normal and we are learning to accept it and embrace it!

Mike has one more week and then it is chemo time again. Please pray that he will enjoy this week and not dread what is ahead! Also, pray that his blood counts will continue to be good. We do not need any delays or interruptions in treatment. His back is feeling much better, but still feels a little weird. Please pray that it will continue to improve and be well before next week hits.

Learning to accept my "new normal"...

## He Sees IT All...

*"I lift up my eyes to the hills—*
*where does my help come from?*
*My help comes from the LORD,*
*the Maker of heaven and earth.*
*He will not let your foot slip—*
*he who watches over you will not slumber;*
*indeed, he who watches over Israel*
*will neither slumber nor sleep.*
*The LORD watches over you—*
*the LORD is your shade at your right hand;*
*the sun will not harm you by day,*
*nor the moon by night.*
*The LORD will keep you from all harm—*
*he will watch over your life;*
*the LORD will watch over your coming and going*
*both now and forevermore."*
Psalm 121:1-8

What a blessing to know that God sees it all! Not just the present, but the future as well. As I was praying this morning asking God to make Mike's blood counts improve so that he can start chemo on Monday, I heard the Holy Spirit whisper "what if it is best for chemo to start later...what if it is best, in the long run, for you to travel to Duke on a different time table than was originally planned." I am reminded that sometimes my prayers need only consist of a heartfelt declaration that I completely trust the Lord and His sovereignty and love. Should I always pray and plead with the Lord to "correct" things when they don't match up with my plans or my wisdom, or should I first pray for wisdom and peace to believe that His will is being done? After all, He knows our needs before we do and He knows the plans He has for us. We have prayed and asked God to provide our every need and to heal Mike. Maybe now, our prayers should reflect our confidence in God and our faith in Him.

He sees it all...from a much broader perspective than we could ever see. Mike's life is in His hands. If God needs Mike to start chemo on Monday in order for His will to be accomplished then he will start chemo on Monday! Otherwise, we trust completely that our prayers have been answered according to God's will. Nothing in all of heaven and earth can thwart the plans God sets in motion.

It can be so difficult to set aside our selfish, human desires. Emotions can so easily cloud our perspective. How sweet of the Holy Spirit to blow in this morning and sweep away the emotions of frustration and worry to help me see things from His perspective. I just love Him so!!!!! There is such great value in being still...in finding moments where God has our full and undivided attention. Unfortunately, there are many "things" in this world that distract me and I am quite often selfish with my time and to what or to whom I give my attention. Thankfully, God is often relentless, and He goes to great lengths to capture my attention and orchestrate moments where He has my undivided affection and focus. It is good to be still!

**In the Stillness....**

Oh sleepless night
My faithful friend
Here we are again

In silence we sit, nothing to say
Senseless thinking
Longing for sweet dreams

Surrounded by darkness
Shadows speak
Taunting...tempting...Ready to devour

Lord, burst forth in light
Rescue my heart
Command my enemy leave

Jesus, sing over me
Sweet songs of love
The sound of victory
Satan's most dreaded tune

Your lullaby calms my heart
It scatters all fears
My eyes grow heavy
My heart is calm
Resting in your love, Lord
It soon will be dawn

Sleepless nights
I no longer dread
Moments with Jesus
My soul is fed

# *Hidden...*

Mike is beginning to feel the effects of this round of chemo. It is getting more and more difficult to get out of bed in the morning. He takes his chemo as close to bedtime as possible with hopes that he will fall asleep quickly in order to escape the dreaded nausea!!!! With the last round, the effects really kicked in Thursday, and the weekend was rough. Please join me in praying for perseverance and stamina to get him through the rest of this round. Pray also that he fixes his eyes on the "finish line", remembering that this is temporary and that he will feel better soon.

My morning devotion came from *Streams in the Desert*[7]. Beautiful words and a reminder that even the worst of our struggles are blessings and valuable, necessary steps in our journey of faith.

*"Dear child, you have had enough of this hurried pace, excitement, and publicity. Now I want you to go and hide yourself – 'hide in the Kerith Ravine' of sickness, the 'Kerith Ravine' of sorrow, or some place of total solitude, from which the crowds have turned away." And happy is the person who can reply to the Lord, 'I long to dwell in your tent forever and take refuge in the shelter of your wings' [Ps. 61:4]. Every saintly soul that desires to wield great influence over others must first win the power in some hidden 'Kerith Ravine.' Acquiring spiritual power is impossible unless we hide from others and ourselves in some deep ravine where we may absorb the power of the Eternal God. May our lives be like the vegetation centuries ago that absorbed the power of the sunshine and now gives the energy back after having become coal."*

As I read these words, I couldn't help but think about Mike. I worry sometimes that being so isolated will cause him to grow depressed and down-hearted. He misses the interaction and relationships with his co-workers (especially his buddy Kent and those clowns Jeff and Jared!!!!! love you guys). I worry that he feels forsaken and alone. This morning, I am reminded that he is never alone and, to be honest, I am slightly jealous as I imagine him tucked away in his "Kerith Ravine", soaking in the radiance of God's glory and grace. I

93

cannot wait to see what God's purpose is in having Mike so tightly tucked away into this dwelling place of solitude...absorbing the power of the Most High, eternal God. And...like the plants that stay buried and become coal, Mike's life will one day be fuel that God uses to allow His plans and power to become a blaze...a fire that ignites a revival in this world to expand His kingdom.

Here is how my devotion ended this morning...such a sweet and gentle reminder for my soul...manna to sustain me today! *"So none of us is exempt from a 'ravine' experience, where the sounds of human voices are exchanged for the waters of quietness that flow from the throne of God, and where we taste sweetness and soak up the power of a life 'hidden in Christ' [Col. 3:3]"*

Don't fear the ravines in your life! Know that, even though it is dark and mysterious, and even a bit creepy, it is a safe place...a place of growth and grace. Thank you, Lord, for providing us a safe place...in the cleft of the rock...where we can gaze upon your glory...and unlike Moses, stare straight into your beautiful face and loving eyes.

**Hidden.........**

Hide me now within your love
Speak the language of your heart

Hold me close; lift my head
I long for your embrace

Steal me away from the chaos of life
Till only you I find

Love so sweet; times of retreat
Calming my anxious mind

94

Peace like no other place
Here and only here
I can clearly see your face

In the cleft I long to dwell
Hiding in Your love....

## *Life Is Like A Box Of Chocolates.....*

The wisdom of Forrest Gump!!!! Waking up today...I had no idea what type of "chocolate" I would be picking from the box. The kids left early with Mike's mom and dad to head to Dollywood. Needless to say...I was wide awake when I could have been sleeping in. I got up and decided to get a few errands done before settling in to accomplish some school work that I am behind on. Now for the rest of the story.......

As I was driving home from Wally World, some kind, conscientious driver decided to cross the yellow line forcing me to swerve into a ditch...well...only half of me ended up in the ditch...the other side of my car stayed on the road and the undercarriage of my van got a nice scraping....and my right front tire was punctured. Can I put this piece of chocolate back in the box and pick another one more to my liking?

So, Lord, what did you have in mind when you saw fit to allow this little trial into my life? Could it be that you realize I am a ticking time bomb of emotions and if I don't release some of this stress, I am going to explode? Hmmmmm...maybe! I have to admit, it felt good to cry! If I wouldn't have hurt myself, I would have probably put my fist through the wall!!! This little unexpected adventure must have been the drop that made my bucket of emotions overflow. I feel much better now! I made it home before my tire deflated, changed the tire, and dropped the van off at the dealership to determine the extent of the damage. Think they would just keep my van and let me keep the Accord they gave me as a loaner....I LIKE IT!!!!! Probably not!

95

Mike is feeling better today. Last night was rough. He was up several times tossing his cookies. His nausea is better this afternoon. If this month is similar to last, he should be feeling a lot better in a few days. Tonight is his last dose of chemo for this round. He is such a trooper!

*"So we fix our eyes not on what is seen, but on what is unseen, since what is seen is temporary, but what is unseen is eternal."* II Cor 4:18.

It is difficult sometimes to not be overwhelmed by the challenges we are facing. Like today...I have to be honest and admit, my first response was..."ARE YOU KIDDING ME? REALLY, LORD? As if we don't already have enough trouble!" Nevertheless...I am OK...I had a good cry...and it is all going to be OK. My eyes were distracted for a moment, and I began to focus on the temporary trial, rather than the eternal unseen. Life is full of those moments. We get slammed by a wave of pain...fear...frustration...loss...and our perspective shifts to the here and now. It happens! And...we can stay there, or we can call out to the Lord and He will take our face in His hands and say..."look at Me...listen to Me...it is all going to be OK! I'm here...it's OK...take a deep breath."

### Breath of Heaven...

Breath of heaven; fill my life
Fall on me like a soft mist
My heart has wandered
My flesh is weak
Let me hear you speak

Gaze into my eyes
Tell me everything will be alright
Cast out my fears with your glorious light

96

Don't let me go under
When waves come crashing in
I know you're my life line
But the tether feels thin

Could we just float down a stream, Lord
Could we just rest a while
To feel your breath like a gentle breeze
That sure would make my heart smile

Breath of heaven
You give life to me
Your love is eternal
Help me to breathe!

## Catching Our Breath...

WOW...it has been a challenging few days. Mike had a pretty rough weekend and was still having problems with nausea and throwing up last night. He went to the doctor today. His platelets were good but white blood counts were down (the lowest they have been) and most likely they will drop even lower over the next weeks. The worst of the nausea seems to hit him at night around bed time. That makes for a long night.

I have been feeling the stress the past few days. I think life is so hectic that even small changes seem to throw us out of rhythm and magnifies the chaos. My favorite way to deal with stress is to hibernate and get away from everyone...not easy to accomplish these days!!!! It takes a lot of energy for me to stay out of the pit. Wow...is this post a downer or what...LOL! I need to spend some time with my friends Peace and Quiet! Good days and bad days...they are just part of the scenery along this unfamiliar path.  I guess we are entitled to a few bad days here and there! Nothing a bite of chocolate or a bowl of ice cream can't fix!

Please pray for Mike's blood counts to hang in there and for his doctors to figure out how to get the nausea and vomiting under control. Pray for Davis...he is so intuitive and takes on our stress. Pray for me to be able to manage my stress. Mal is doing great...pray that we are able to discern her needs...she is good at "hiding" things and holding them in. Thank you all for your love and prayers. Your fervent prayers are powerful and effective and we feel them lifting us up!!!!! We selfishly ask that you remember us and respond to the Holy Spirit's call to share words of encouragement! We rely on them daily!!!!!

## Safe...

*"Strength will rise as we wait upon the Lord...our God...You reign forever...our hope...our strong deliverer...You are the everlasting God...You do not faint...You won't grow weary...You're the defender of the weak...You comfort those in need...You lift us up on wings like eagles."*[9]

I have been singing this song in my head all day long! Finally...I feel like the Lord has swooped in and lifted me on His wings to soar above the stress and ever mounting heap of responsibilities!!!! AND IT FEELS WONDERFUL! BUT...I have had to work so hard to be still...to cease striving! I've had to constantly remind myself that those who wait upon the Lord, who sit still rather than running around like a chicken with its head cut off...will find strength...His strength...as they tap into His power...they will soar even in the midst of trials...for He is carrying them...we will walk along the long, lonely, and even treacherous path and not grow faint...because He walks with us and leads us and provides drinks of His thirst quenching Living Water.

I thought about some of the things that prevent me from being still sometimes. One picture that God brought into my mind was when I fell and broke my shoulder. My first reaction was to jump up, go about my business, and ignore the pain. However, once I sat still, I realized there was something terribly wrong and I was in a great deal of pain. Ignoring my pain and brokenness could only last for a short while...eventually it became unbearable and I had to seek help.

I also thought about how Mallory often responds to pain. She has had numerous crashes on her bike. She does not ignore the pain, but she works herself into a tizzy and even though she runs to Mike or me for help, it is quite a task for us to calm her down and remind or convince her that she is OK and that we are going to take care of her.

Finally, I thought about the times when I have fallen into the trap of trying to fix things and relying on my own ability and wearing myself out when I should have ceased striving and sought the Lord's wisdom and help, reminding myself of the truths found in His word. Even though my problem may not be solved immediately, my spirit could be soaring with Him above the stress and strain of what was going on.

The past week has been a rough one...one that I had no chance of "fixing". My only way out was to go through it and endure it. I will admit that there were times I felt weary and faint. But, as I waited upon the Lord, He renewed my strength and enabled me to run when needed and walk steadily at other times...and now my heart is soaring. When we wait...be still...cease striving...we create opportunities for God to be exalted...either in our hearts alone, or in our hearts and in the world around us. Focusing on His greatness and glory...being still long enough to catch a glimpse of His majesty...is what causes us to soar.

*"but those who hope in the LORD will renew their strength. They will soar on wings like eagles; they will run and not grow weary, they will walk and not be faint." Isaiah 40:31*

*"Be still, and know that I am God; I will be exalted among the nations, I will be exalted in the earth." Psalm 46:10*

Wow...it is so hard sometimes to be still...to cease striving...and to just allow God to bring me through a trial. In my flesh, I'll be honest and say that I'd much rather take a detour...but I sure don't want to miss the spectacular view that is found on this unfamiliar path!!!!! A clear and glorious view of His beauty and grace!

**Safe...**

Working
Striving
Worn out and weak
Walking
Trudging
Running from pain

Breathless
Fainting
Confused and forlorn
Be still my soul
Stop and behold...

I see in the distance
A great glorious glow
Coming closer and closer
I Feel its warmth

Jesus, sweet Jesus
He's come to my aid
"Climb on" He says
Rest in my care

There's no need to worry
No need to fret
Be still my child
You're going to be safe!

Yes...I am safe!

# *Safe In His Arms...*

We lost a dear friend and church family member, Betty Standifer. Almost two years ago, Betty was diagnosed with the same cancer that Mike has. She was so full of courage and determination during her battle to beat cancer. We are eternally grateful to the Standifer/Brown family for the encouragement and wisdom they shared with us when we began our journey.

II Corinthians 1:3-7 says, *"All praise to God, the Father of our Lord Jesus Christ. God is our merciful Father and the source of all comfort. He comforts us in all our troubles so that we can comfort others. When they are troubled, we will be able to give them the same comfort God has given us. For the more we suffer for Christ, the more God will shower us with his comfort through Christ. Even when we are weighed down with troubles, it is for your comfort and salvation! For when we ourselves are comforted, we will certainly comfort you. Then you can patiently endure the same things we suffer. We are confident that as you share in our sufferings, you will also share in the comfort God gives us."* NLT

Betty and her family embraced Paul's words and determined in their hearts that her suffering would not be in vain. They were an instrument of comfort that God used to touch our lives when we realized the path God was taking us on. Betty is with Jesus now, and He has wiped away her last tear. She will only know comfort now...no pain...no fear...no sickness...only life!

One of my favorite quotes from Amy Carmichael[5] says, "What will it be like to see Him whom I have known so long, but never seen? To adore His beauty; to worship Him in holiness? ...What will it be like, when faith and hope fade out of sight...and only Love is left?" Betty knows the answer to this question, for her...only love remains! She is safe in His arms!

101

**Safe in His arms...**

Once alone and in the dark
My heart had no home
Then Jesus came calling
And I invited Him in

We walked life together
Hand in hand
Over mountains
Through valleys
He was my closest friend

There were constant reminders
Of His unending love
How precious my Savior
How peaceful my heart

As time passed me by
Moments of joy and delight
I soon came to notice
They paled in His light

Though my life has been blessed here
Nothing will ever compare
To the moment I see Him
To the moment I rest

I no longer yearn
I no longer dream
I am safe in His arms now and I forever will live

In memory of Betty Standifer...a beautiful picture of a heart and life completely devoted to Jesus. No doubt she heard her Savior say..."well done my good and faithful servant...well done...now forever enter my rest."

## *Instruments Of Love...*

A few years ago, I received a copy of a little book titled *I Come Quietly to Meet You*[5], which I have already referenced several times in my postings. It contains a collection of Amy Carmichael's writing. Amy was a pioneer...one of the things I admire about her most. I quickly fell in love with her heart. In the late 1800's Amy set out on her own to serve as a missionary in India. She ended up risking her life in order to save young boys and girls who were kept as slaves and prostitutes at Hindu temples. Her life was threatened on many accounts, but God protected her and used her in a mighty way. Another thing I admire about Amy is that she spent the last 20 years of her life bedridden after a crippling accident. It was during this time that she wrote many of her timeless devotions and reflections of God's goodness and love. Think about it...20 years stuck in a bed in the mid 1900's in India pouring out her heart on paper as a result of knowing, truly knowing that God was good and that, despite her trials and hardships (and they were truly hardships), He loved her and longed to bless her.

Amy was blessed to have discovered the depths of God's heart. During her affliction, she tucked herself into God and learned to abide in His amazing love. In her writings, she mentions her deep longing to leave this world, to be delivered from her suffering and to be with Christ once and for all. She knew she was just passing through this world and that her ultimate treasure would be to leave this world behind and one day meet Jesus face to face. The pleasures and comforts of this world would no longer satisfy and steal her attention from Him. Though still in this world physically, Amy's heart was already in heaven and all the treasures of this world paled in comparison to the thought of one day being with her King - forever. Amy was truly an instrument of love. She sacrificed so much of her life and gave so much in order that others might have a better life. Even when she was confined to a bed, her mission to proclaim the name of Christ and bring glory to God ruled her life.

This past week, our church family said good-bye to an instrument of God's love. However, she has left a legacy that will endure...a legacy of love...God's perfect love. She has now seen the one she has known for so long but never seen. She is forever adoring His beauty and worshiping Him in perfect holiness. Faith and hope have faded out of sight...no longer necessary...and now...only love...perfect love is left. Love...the one thing that endures all things - even death.

Could the trials and suffering of this world possibly be FOR OUR BENEFIT? Certainly! It is through the most painful of trials that the power of God's love is able to work to its fullest potential. Trials are also an instrument of His love. The question is...will we invite Him and His love into our pain?

Amy Carmichael seized the benefits of her suffering by inviting God to speak to her heart and use her in spite of her earthly limitations. Our earthly limitations are no match for God's sovereign purpose. I wonder if, after all these year of basking in His glory, that Amy Carmichael wonders how her devotion to Christ might still be touching people's lives today? It is certainly touching mine!

*"No one's ever seen or heard anything like this, Never so much as imagined anything quite like it— What God has arranged for those who love him."*
*I Cor 2:9 The Message*

Although it is not always easy, Mike and I long to seize the benefits of our suffering, and we realize that the true benefits are that we learn more about the heart of God. We see Him more clearly and accurately. We trust Him more. We long for the day (and yes...hope that it is not anytime soon) that only love is left. Until then, we will strive to be instruments of His love.

# Behind The Clouds And Fog...

The kids and I receive a special treat on our drive to school almost every morning. As we arrive at the crest of a hill, we come to an opening in the trees and houses that usually reveals a spectacular view of the sunrise. We have gotten to the point now that we anticipate the view and opportunity to marvel at God's beautiful creation and reminder that His mercies are new every morning...just as the sun rises and brings light and hope...His mercies do the same.

This morning, we drove to work in a thick dense fog and were not able to see even a hint of the sunrise. Although disappointing, God reminded me that even when the fog and clouds of life roll in...behind them His light still shines and He is still King of all creation and the Creator of our hearts! Even though our "view" of God becomes blocked or dulled by the trials of life (clouds/fog), the truth still remains...He is there...AND...though our "view" of Him may be blocked, there is NEVER a moment that He does not see us! It is in those moments that we must bring more focus and attention to each "step" we take...we must dig deeper into our faith and allow our complete and total trust in the Lord to guide us. The "clouds and fog" of life should cause us to focus more intently on what we know and trust about our faithful God...reaching to Him, taking His hand, and allowing Him to lead and guide us.

Just because there are clouds and fog and we cannot see the sunrise, mountains, or stars does not mean they are not there...they are...and so is our loving Savior! *"Be strong and courageous. Do not be afraid or terrified because of them, for the LORD your God goes with you; he will never leave you nor forsake you" Deuteronomy 31:6*

Mike is beginning to feel a bit better. He was able to receive his Avastin treatment yesterday. His blood work was actually better than they had expected - whites came up a bit, platelets and reds were down a bit but within normal range. They had expected his whites to drop even more than they had...praise the Lord they actually went up! He also found out that round two of chemo is the round they use to evaluate the dosages of Topotecan (the second chemo). Depending on how the patient tolerates the meds in round two gives them an indication of what dosage adjustments need to be made. His nurse specialist at Thompson told him that the protocol he is currently on is pretty aggressive. It may be that Duke adjusts the dosage when we go back for Mike's next follow-up next week. We would appreciate your prayers as we head to Duke. Pray for another "beautiful" MRI, wisdom, and just an overall fabulous report!

# *Your Story...*

The God who created you is El Roi – the God who sees. The names of God that begin with "El" refer to God's awesome power and might. It is by His awesome power and deity that He is able to see EVERYTHING at every moment. He is all knowing...all powerful...always present. Do you need to know God as El Roi right now? He is the **God who sees** what you or someone you care about is going through! Call out to the God who sees you and listen for His still small voice to answer...He is faithful and He will answer you from His holy hill...He will lift your head in His loving hands until your eyes look into His and He will gently whisper, "It is all O.K. I am here! I am your Healer and the God who sees it all!"

Chapter Eight

# *Our Every Need...*

*"And my God will supply all your needs according to His riches in glory in Christ Jesus." Philippians 4:19 HCSB*

It was difficult to believe that Mike had already finished two rounds of treatment and we were ready to head back to Duke for another checkup and MRI.  As we prepared to go, we were both rather confident that the MRI will be clean.  At least it had better be.  If not, we knew that Mike was in trouble.  If there had been tumor growth at this point that meant one thing...the cancer was winning and the treatments were not achieving what we had hoped they would.  The reality of Mike's situation was unavoidable, but we did our very best not dwell on the gravity of the situation and prognosis – only by the grace of God.  He had truly been a shield and fortress protecting our hearts and minds. We had managed to dwell within His shelter and rest in His shadow (Ps. 91).  He's a huge God and He casts a big shadow! We continued to place our trust in Him and we felt our faith growing day by day, week by week. As God showered our lives with His grace, we were finding the nourishment we needed to grow strong enough to withstand the winds that blew continually throughout this storm.

So...we were off...back to Duke! We felt a strange mixture of perfect peace and anxiety. We were ready!

## Redeeming Love...

Thanks for all the prayers and encouragement this week. Mike and I are very excited to get away this weekend and celebrate our anniversary. Many of you have known us from the start of our life together. For those of you who have not...let me just say...it has been quite a journey. I can't pass up an opportunity to use this public platform to say a very public thank you to my wonderful husband. He has loved me so unconditionally for 20 years...and much of the time, I did not deserve to be loved! He has been so patient, so kind, so faithful, so strong, such a godly example to me, our children, and so many others. Love is such a special gift. Marriage should paint a beautiful picture to the world of Christ's love for His bride...the church. Although our marriage has not been perfect, I can honestly say that our love is strengthened by the cord of God's love and grace. I know Mike would agree, we would probably not be married today if it weren't for the work God has done in our lives and in our hearts. Only by His grace did we awaken to our deep need for Him and the realization that He is the only thing that will truly satisfy our souls. When we are satisfied in and by Him, everything else falls into place! So...to my wonderful husband...thank you...I love you very much!

**Redeeming Love...**

*You saw in my heart what I could not see*
*Your sure and gentle love I'd soon come to know*

*20 years have come and gone*
*A beautiful journey...a beautiful song!*

*Out of the blue you entered my life*
*God's blessed gift*
*Love of my life*

*Young and unknowing*
*Blind leading the blind*
*God had a purpose revealed in due time*

*Covered by grace*
*He has faithfully led*
*At times never knowing the touch of His hand*
*Mountains and valleys*
*Rejoicing and grief*
*Each step was sovereign we now clearly see*

*Your love changed my life*
*A safe place to be*

111

*Forgiveness, acceptance, and mercy*
*God's love shown to me*

*How can I ever thank you*
*How can I ever express*
*Just how much I love you*
*Just how much I've been blessed*
*Redeeming love*
*God's beautiful design*
*Two lives surrendered*
*Two hearts intertwined*

*20 years behind us*
*Many more to come*
*What adventures await us*
*What will deepen our love*

*As I stop and reflect*
*On our journey thus far*
*My heart overflows*
*I'm overwhelmed by God's love*

## Round 2...

Well...we made it to Duke this evening and we are all rested and relaxed after a weekend in the North Carolina mountains. We had an absolutely wonderful weekend driving on the Blue Ridge Parkway, enjoying time with friends, a wonderful morning of worship, a beautiful day to tour Biltmore...a fabulous celebration of 20 amazing years together. Mike has an MRI tomorrow morning at 10:00am. After that he will see the doctors at the Duke brain tumor center around 1:00pm. Our last stop will be meeting with the clinical trial coordinator around 2:30

or 3:00pm and then we head back to Knoxville. We are both a bit anxious about the day.

We are praying and hoping for another "beautiful" MRI, trusting completely in God's grace and love. Our knees are a bit shaky, but our feet are firmly planted on the Rock. I was just thinking today as we were driving to Durham...there is absolutely no way of explaining WHY we are in this nightmare, but regardless of our lack of knowing "why", we do have so many answers and truths to cling to! We thank God that He has given us the faith to move beyond trying to answer all the "why's" to just accepting this and living out the "why"...looking for opportunities for God to reveal glimpses of the "why" according to His perfect will. Ultimately our "why's" can be satisfied with "for My glory". Knowing and trusting that God is good, loving, and faithful makes all the "why's", "if's", and "what if's" bearable and less frustrating. Tis so sweet to trust in Jesus...just to take Him at His word...

We appreciate your prayers for us as we head into tomorrow and for all the prayers and petitions made regarding our weekend...It was exceedingly and abundantly more than we could have ever asked for or imagined!!!!!!

Trusting...

## *The Cry Of Our Hearts...*

### When Words Just Won't Do...

In times like these words just aren't enough
to express what I feel in my heart

Your joy, your grace, your tender touch
Your mercy and faithfulness

Lord why have you chosen to bless us so
How could we possibly deserve

113

Such a wonderful life
Such extravagant love
Such an enormous measure of grace

You're ever near
We feel your embrace
We gaze into your face
No darkness
No fear

Confident in You
Our hearts are bold and strong
Words just can't express how thankful we are
No language could ever convey
The depths of our awe
The gratitude we feel
The wonders and glory we see

But words are not needed
No not even one
You've given us a way to say "thank you"
When words just won't do
We open our hearts
And you hear every heartfelt cry

WOW...how can we even begin to express what we are feeling in our hearts? It wouldn't be possible. We are so thrilled to have gotten another good report and clean MRI today. I'd be lying if I said we were not nervous going into this visit to Duke. When we heard to words "your MRI looks great" the doctor could have just stopped there!

There are no words in the human vocabulary that could accurately express our joy and our thankfulness to God. What a relief to know that He created and knows the language of our hearts. We can merely lift our hearts to Him and allow them to express every thought and feeling we long to convey to our wonderful Lord.

Many of those thoughts and feelings concern you! Today, as we sat in the examination room, I read this verse and thought of each of you...our faithful prayer warriors..."*...On Him we have set our hope that He will continue to deliver us, as you help us by your prayers. Then many will give thanks on our behalf for the gracious favor granted to us in answer to the prayers of many" II Cor. 1:10-11*. As you pray for us, and as God answers those prayers, the attention of so many is turned towards our wonderful Lord bringing Him much glory and honor and praise...as others see Him working in Mike's life. Your prayers go far beyond helping our family and easing Mike's suffering...they cause others to see the glory, faithfulness, and power of the Lord. For us...that is the greatest blessing of all! He and He alone deserves the glory and honor and praise!!!!

Join us in praising and thanking Him! Join us in proclaiming His greatness so that others might see and know that He is the Lord of the universe and that He desires to be intimately involved in the lives of those He created.

In awe of His love...

## Puzzles...

Our daughter, Mallory, loves jigsaw puzzles...even the really big ones with hundreds of tiny pieces that all look the same. Last Christmas, Mike's staff gave us a "Smokey Mountain" goodie basket and one of the items in it was a beautiful puzzle that pictured the wildlife of the Smokey Mountains. Mallory could not wait to work on the puzzle. I, on the other hand, dreaded it!!!! I am much too "ADD" to work jigsaw puzzles. I'm fine with putting the edge pieces together, but once you get down to working with all the pieces that look just alike...I'm done! Anyway, Mal worked and worked on that puzzle. Towards the end, rather than getting frustrated and giving up, she would walk into the dining room and look over the pieces...if she was able to place a piece fine...if not...fine...she would just carry on and come back another time. Other times, she would sit and study the pieces for a length of time. Sometimes placing a piece in its proper spot...sometimes not. I was amazed by her patience and persistence. She knew the pieces fit together and she knew that eventually she would figure out HOW. She was patient enough to persevere and, finally, she would get to enjoy the reward of seeing the final picture and its beauty. To her...that was a goal worth pursuing.

A few days ago, for some reason, I recalled how much I loved playing in the rain as a child. Walking outside barefoot, splashing in the puddles of water that pooled up against the curb...looking for worms...maybe even making a few mud pies. I have no idea why I thought about that. I don't really remember another time that I have thought about or reminisced about playing in the rain. But...it was a sweet memory that made my heart smile. Today, as we were driving to church, I heard a beautiful song on the radio that talked about rejoicing and praising God even in the storms of life. Instantly, the vision of playing in the rain as a little girl entered my mind. It was as if these two puzzle pieces had instantly fit together giving me a much clearer picture of God's work in my life. A reminder that I can experience that same feeling as I did when I was a little girl if I will now dance and splash around in the shower of God's love and grace in the midst of this storm.

Life is not a series of random events. God, in His sovereignty, is working to complete the work He has begun. If we take the time to study the puzzle pieces of life...either from past to present or day to day...we are much more likely to see God's plans and purpose taking shape. We are much more likely to see the details of our life from His perspective. In doing so, we remain aware of and focused on the fact that HE IS the one putting the pieces of our life puzzle together...HE IS involved in the details and circumstances of our life. Our lives do not have to be hundreds of random puzzle pieces that lay in a box on the shelf or in the closet. We can ask God to show us how they fit

116

together...how each event is linked together...what purpose it serves. He is the Potter, we are the clay....or...He is the Puzzle Worker...we are the puzzle. He is intimately aware of every circumstance and puzzle piece of our life! What a comfort there is in knowing and believing that truth! THAT is what allows us to be still and KNOW that He is God and that He is with us and for us and fighting for us! He is such an awesome God!

God is a detailed God...He has plans and a purpose for our life, and those plans involve opportunities for His amazing power and glory to be displayed. My puzzle is not finished yet, but I know the challenges my family is facing right now are somehow going to fit into place in a way that will eventually reveal a beautiful picture of God's amazing love and grace. What a mighty God we serve!

Tomorrow is a big day. Mike's platelets need to be up to 100 in order for him to start this round of chemo. They were at 89 Friday. He has been eating kale all weekend. In fact, I came home from running some errands this afternoon and found him eating a BOWL of kale drenched in ranch dressing! Hey...you do what ya gotta do! Please pray for God's will to be done and for us to have peace and confidence that He is in control and aware of our every need and fully capable of and willing to move heaven and earth in order for His will to be done. Seeing more clearly...

## So Far So Good...

"Our God is so big so strong and so mighty...there's nothing our God cannot do!" YAY...platelets are up to 141 and Mike is staying on track. He had an Avastin treatment this morning and will start chemo tonight. Our new motto is...we love kale! We love Jesus more though and thank Him for giving us kale if that is what caused his platelets to increase!!!! So far, Mike is feeling pretty good. He started feeling nauseated last night and took some of his new anti-nausea meds and they seemed to keep it at bay. Considering the last two rounds, the worst is yet to come. If the pattern holds true, tomorrow is when the nausea will begin to hit the hardest. BUT...we are praying that the new anti-nausea meds will be more effective and a new pattern will be established.

Thank you all so very much for praying. God is so incredibly merciful and good.  Regardless of our circumstances...He is good and His grace is sufficient. I hope and pray that each of you will experience His grace in a new and special way and that your days will be filled with glimpses of His glory!

Oh...and I would like to ask you to pray for Lisa Smith.  She lives in Maryville, TN and was diagnosed with GBM brain cancer near the time that Mike was. She is finishing up radiation this next week and is going to need an extra measure of grace and strength to push to the finish line. Please pray for her, her husband Mark, and their children. They are such a precious family and it has been a blessing for our family to meet them and for us to encourage one another.

Time for more kale....

# *A Skip In His Step...*

Praise the Lord!!!! This month has been much easier for Mike in terms of negative side effects. It seems as though the new anti-nausea medicine has been helpful. Mike was still nauseated from the chemo; however, he did not throw up and he was able to maintain a much more substantial diet. He is already feeling so much better and last night and tonight he ate a pretty normal meal (instead of pasta, potatoes, or rice).

The improvement has been such an encouragement for Mike. I can tell his spirit is so much more upbeat and positive...he just feels so much better! I cannot even begin to tell you how happy I am to see Mike feeling so well. I do not think he has felt this good since all this craziness started. His color is good, his energy is good, and he has a little skip in his step. Such a blessing! He had an Avastin treatment on Monday. His blood counts were GREAT. Platelets were the highest they have been since starting treatment. They generally bottom out two weeks or so after chemo, but we are hopeful that the trend will improve this month.

Kale is now a staple in our home.

## *Lost In His Love...*

I am overwhelmed by God's love today! Not sure why. Just a sweet sappy feeling in my heart. During homeroom, I was sharing with my students about God's redeeming love and its power to overcome the worst of shame, pain, and anything else that comes as a result of sin. We watched a video of Christian recording artist and song writer Heather William's testimony on YouTube. I felt overcome by the Holy Spirit and the truth He poured into my heart as I shared with my students. God's grace is so amazing. It is truly the medicine for our every need. For forgiveness, strength, comfort, healing, peace...whatever we need...His grace is sufficient! I feel like I have had more than my fair share of grace! Throughout my life, God has poured out His grace lavishly...even before I knew Him...He was singing over me...calling my heart to come and receive His love. Only by His grace was I able to come.

Cancer has been hard on our family...but God has been mighty!!!! Evidence of His grace can be found in every area of our lives! At times we feel so lost in this new and unknown place, but...we are lost in His love and that is a great place to be!

**Lost in His Love...**

The sun shone bright all around us
No warning
Now surrounded by a terrible storm

Thunder
Lightning
A sudden down pour

119

Where to run
Where to hide
Seeking shelter we found ourselves by Your side

Calmness
Safety
Now lost in Your love

The storm still rages
The winds come and go
Thunder rumbles in the distance
A constant reminder of the storm

Flashes of lightening cast fears and doubts
As we see more clearly
Our helplessness

Speak, Lord
Command the storm to flee
With one word from you
It must obey

Sing over us, Jesus
Drown out the sounds
Doubts, confusion, fear
Their taunting voice we hear

You are our shelter firm and secure
Our stronghold, our hope
So, let the storm rage
Let the winds blow

A new place we've found
A place that we choose
A place of sweet rest
We are lost in Your love
No better place to be

## No Greater Love...

There is no greater love in this world than the love of God! In fact, at times, I find it quite overwhelming. Not overwhelming in the sense that it makes me uncomfortable...overwhelming in the sense that I cannot possibly understand and fully grasp the depth and magnitude of it. In spite of all I've been and all that I still am...He chooses to love me so deeply and bless me so generously. After all...He IS love...He cannot be anything apart from love...it is who God is....not what He chooses to do...He is perfect, holy love!

Sunday, Mike was asked to say a few words to our church family about our journey. I was so incredibly proud of him. As difficult as this journey is for me, it must be exponentially difficult for him. I try to understand, but I am not sure if it is possible to walk in his shoes and experience what he is going through. He is so strong, determined, and disciplined. He has such faith and genuine love for God. He is truly an inspiration to me and to so many of you, I am sure.

As I sat in church Sunday, I thought about the many ways that God has blessed my family over the past 6 months. I thought to myself *how in the world can I ever thank you, Lord, for the outpouring of your grace on my life?* The only thing I came up with was that I could live my life as a constant prayer of thanksgiving to God...ever aware of His presence, grace, and mercy...ever aware of and responding to His touch...with words of praise continually on my lips and in my heart.

**Lord...let my life be a prayer to you...**

In my heart are many treasures
Ways you've touched my life
Your love, compassion, mercy, and grace
I've done nothing to deserve

Yet you come, Lord; You embrace me
You wipe away the dirt and tears
What words could ever fully express
The gratitude of my heart

It seems impossible although I try, Lord
Only hoping you really know
Just how much I adore you...just how much I need your love

If I were to tell of every blessing
Of all that you've done in me
I'd forever be singing of your great love
From now to the ends of this age

But I'll try, Lord
I'll keep singing your praise
I'll shout for the world to know

Your glory
Your power
Your faithfulness
Your grace
Lord, let my life be a constant prayer

# Round 4...

It is difficult to believe that Mike will be starting round 4 of his treatments this coming week. Well...hopefully! On Friday, his platelets had continued to drop and were down to 71. They need to be at 100 or he will not be able to start another round of chemo or take Avastin. Please pray for God's will and perfect timing. Pray that we will have faith in and peace from knowing that God is sovereign, in control, and faithful to hear and answer our prayers. So...come what may Monday...we say in advance..."thank you, Lord". Thanks for faithfully praying and for continuing to love us, support us, care for us, and walk with us on this journey.

Thankful...

# The Door To Doubt and Fear...

Just a quick update to let you all know what is going on. Mike had his blood checked today and his platelets were at 90. Not sure why he has not rebounded. His nurse at Thompson called Duke and they want him to wait until Friday to have his blood checked again. If his platelets are up on Friday, then he will start chemo on Monday.

God promises that when we pray we will have whatever we ask in Jesus name. We have prayed and He has answered according to His will. What peace we find in knowing that He is in control and sees the big picture. The frustration and desire to stay on track with treatments leaves an open door for doubt and fear. But, Mike and I are both a bit on the stubborn side and we stubbornly choose to stay safely tucked within the shelter of the Most High!!!! Sorry...Satan...you are not allowed in here!!!

Stubbornly trusting Him...

123

# Remaining Hopeful...

I have been thinking a lot today about the peace I feel in my heart. In my mind, I am torn by the fact that Mike did not get to start chemo this week. My flesh is tempting me to fret and complain about the delay. The delay causes a ripple effect in our lives...when will we go to Duke next...how will the change effect our plans for Christmas...is the delay going to minimize the effectiveness of treatment? On the other hand, my heart is calm and confident...confident that God is in control and totally aware of the timing and necessity of treatment...confident that God hears and answers our prayers...confident that He will provide our every need!

Though the questions swirling in our minds cause the waves of doubt to become more prevalent, our hearts are anchored and holding tight to the hope we have in Christ! *"We have this hope as an anchor for the soul, firm and secure. It enters the inner sanctuary behind the curtain, where our forerunner, Jesus, has entered on our behalf..."* *Hebrews 6:19-20.* We don't have a hope that is merely wishful thinking...a hope that is merely a life preserver that keeps us afloat. NO...we have a hope that is firm and secure...an anchor tightly tethered to our great High Priest who is seated on His throne and well aware of our sufferings, fears, doubts, frustrations, etc. Our souls are anchored to Christ who is in the holy of holies, interceding for us...fighting for us...moving heaven and earth to accomplish God's good, pleasing and perfect will. That is the truth...God's Word...His promise...and we choose to believe! In doing so...our peaceful hearts are able to calm our anxious minds!

My hope is built on nothing less
Than Jesus' blood and righteousness;
I dare not trust the sweetest frame,
But wholly lean on Jesus' name.

On Christ, the solid Rock, I stand;
All other ground is sinking sand.

124

When darkness veils His lovely face,
I rest on His unchanging grace;
In every high and stormy gale
My anchor holds within the veil.

On Christ, the solid Rock, I stand;
All other ground is sinking sand.

His oath, His covenant, and blood
Support me in the whelming flood;
When every earthly prop gives way,
He then is all my Hope and Stay.

On Christ, the solid Rock, I stand;
All other ground is sinking sand.

When He shall come with trumpet sound,
Oh, may I then in Him be found,
Clothed in His righteousness alone,
Faultless to stand before the throne!

On Christ, the solid Rock, I stand;
All other ground is sinking sand.[10]

HE is our hope!

## He's An On Time God...

*"Faith is the confidence that what we hope for will actually happen; it gives us assurance about things we cannot see."* Hebrews 11:1 NLT

Faith and hope! Without faith, we have no hope...hope fuels our faith. Two essential ingredients to surviving this journey here on earth.

The question is what are we placing our faith in and what are we hoping for? Clearly, Hebrews 11 tells us that faith in God should give us solid assurance of certain things...but what? Because I hope that Mike's cancer will never return, does that mean that it will not? If it does, did I not have enough faith...was I not confident enough? Of course not! My hope cannot be based on the outcome of my circumstances on this earth, but rather on the eternal outcome of my circumstances and the truth I know about the promises of God. So...what am I HOPING for in this journey? I am hoping that God will be glorified and that His perfect will is done....now that is something I can have faith in and hope for...I am completely confident that it will happen!

Today, I was thinking about the story of Lazarus' death. Mary and Martha sent word to Jesus that Lazarus was sick, but He took His time in getting to Lazarus. In fact, by the time Jesus arrived, Lazarus was dead. However, Jesus had told His disciples that Lazarus' illness would not end in death. Had Jesus been wrong? Did He get distracted and have to change the outcome to prove Himself right? No...Jesus' timing was perfect! He tarried for a reason. What was that reason? *"...for God's glory so that God's Son may be glorified through it"* John 11:4.

God is an on time God!!!! We must believe that! We must trust that! We must have faith in that...so confident in this truth that we are filled with hope and assurance that God's will is being done and that He has not been detained nor forsaken our cries. Jesus tarried so that Lazarus could be raised from the dead and there would be no doubts in the miracle He had performed. In the Jewish culture, it was believed that the spirit lingered over a dead body for three days. Jesus arrived right on time...on the fourth day...in order that no one could say that Lazarus' spirit re-entered His body or that He wasn't really dead. He was dead...and there was no debating it...Jesus brought Lazarus back to life!

Believing that God is an on time God is essential for our family on this journey through cancer. The only thing for sure is that nothing is for sure! We cannot predict from one month to the next how treatment will go...we cannot plan...we cannot schedule our lives more than a week at a time...sometimes a day at a time. But we have faith and complete confidence that what we hope for (God's perfect will) WILL be accomplished...even when it "seems" that things are going terribly wrong from our perspective. He's an on time God...yesterday, today, and tomorrow...He never changes!

# ThankFULL.....

It's the most wonderful time of the year! Seriously! I love this time of year...all of it! The food...the fun...family...the hustle and bustle...the giving...more food...more fun...more family! But most of all, I love the celebration of thankfulness and the days of advent as we ponder thoughts of what it must have been like for Joseph, Mary, and those who waited anxiously for their King...their Savior...to arrive.

I'm sure it comes as no surprise to read that, this year, our family is exceedingly thankful. As you have journeyed with us, you have seen the abundant blessings and answered prayers that we have received. I am not most thankful for what God has done, necessarily, but thankful for WHO God IS and for how He has made Himself known in our lives. As I reflect on the thankfulness in my heart this year, I am keenly aware of the many times throughout my life that my thankfulness has been so selfish, so worldly, and based on the gift, not the Giver. However, this year, my heart is full of gratitude based on nothing more than pure and perfect adoration of God, whose love and faithfulness are worth more than any other gift in this world.

1 Thessalonians 5:18 states that we should *"Be thankful in all circumstances, for this is God's will for you who belong to Christ Jesus."* NLT *(emphasis added).* Regardless of our circumstances, we can choose to be thankful IN them! I will never be thankful for cancer, but each day, I find so many things to be thankful for IN the midst of this journey. It is a choice! The key is to first look at the cross...from this perspective, I cannot help but have a heart full of gratitude and praise. All the darkness of my trials pales in the light of the cross...it casts a glorious glow over my life and in my heart bringing with it joy, peace, thankfulness, confidence, and faith.

I cannot even find words to express my thankfulness this year. Maybe because it is not necessarily attached to any one given "thing". It is just a result of abiding in God's love...a natural response to resting in His grace. So...IN the midst of this storm...I choose to be thankful. Should I dare to say that I am even thankful FOR this circumstance? It may seem crazy, but yes...I am! For it is because of this trial that I have been able to see the tender face of God...the mercy in His eyes...the love in His smile...the power of His touch like never before... and that is truly a gift to cherish and be thankful for! Just plain thankful...

## Testimony Of Faith...

Every day, we have an opportunity to let our lives share a testimony of God's greatness...His love...His faithfulness...His graciousness...His goodness...and so on. What is your life testifying about? Take advantage of the opportunities before you to bring glory to God and help others see that He is the source of your strength...your hope...your faith...your very life! I am so proud of Mike for so beautifully sharing his perspective on this journey and how God has so faithfully sustained our family over the past months. Love you Honey!!!!

**Only a Great and Glorious God...**

Only a great and glorious God
Could touch my heart like You do
You know my thoughts
You know my needs
Intimately caring for me

Only a great and glorious God
Could light up the night like you do
Each twinkling star a reminder
You number the hairs on my head

Only a great and glorious God
Could heal my deepest wounds
There's no need to hide
No need to fear
Your grace is the medicine I need

Only a great and glorious God
Could calm the storms like you do
"Be still" you command
And my heart is at rest
Within the shelter of your wings I can dwell
Only a great and glorious God
Would save us from our sin
We mock You
We betray You
We waste your grace
Yet still...You choose to love

Only a great and glorious God
So huge...So powerful...So wise
Could become small enough
To lay in a manger
To break the curse of sin with His cry

Only a great and glorious God
Would leave heaven for this broken world
Refusing to forsake
You came as a babe
To rescue the hearts of man

Only a great and glorious God
Deserves my attention and love
Only a great and glorious God
Deserves my highest praise!

129

Thank you God for sending your Son to break the silence of the night with His cry...to shatter the chains that held us captive to sin. Thank you for the gift of life that came down from heaven full of grace and truth...Jesus...our Savior...Emmanuel.

I am amazed by the many ways God goes to great lengths to get my attention. Through a sun rise...through a friend...through His word...through His still small voice...He is faithful to remind me each and every day that He is Emmanuel...God with us...God with ME! As I drove to school this morning by myself, God blessed me with the most beautiful sunrise I have ever seen. Seriously...I had to stop and just sit and look at it for a while. Only a great and glorious God would do that...could do that! He knows how much I love a beautiful sunrise and how it makes my heart smile. He is so intimately involved in the details of this world, and more importantly, of our lives. Only a great and glorious God who is so huge could become small enough to speak to our simple, finite minds.

Stop and look for this great and glorious God today! How has He chosen to speak to you? Will you see...will you listen...will you respond? I hope so...great and glorious blessings await you!

Mike is feeling GREAT! We had such a wonderful Thanksgiving. He heads back to Duke next Tuesday. Please join us in praying for another "beautiful" MRI. I am not going with Mike on this trip, which is causing a bit of anxiety for me. He is going with his mom and dad and I am going to stay home with the kids...and Jesus close by my side!

In awe of His glory...

# *Your Story...*

What do you need from God right now? Do you have a physical, tangible need? Do you need to feel His touch? Do you need wisdom? Do you need just enough grace to make it through the day? With a prayerful heart and a thankful spirit (knowing and trusting that He will provide what you NEED), boldly approach His throne of grace with confidence that He will supply your every need through His riches in Christ Jesus your loving Redeemer!

Chapter Nine

# *All I Want For Christmas...*

*"Now to Him who is able to do above and beyond all that we ask or think
—according to the power that works in you— to Him be glory in the
church and in Christ Jesus to all generations,
forever and ever. Amen." Ephesians 3:20-21 HCSB*

Thanksgiving had passed (the holiday, anyway! I suppose every day should be thanksgiving!). Now...I was ready to celebrate Christmas! I LOVE Christmas and everything about the season. I love the hustle and bustle. I love the decorations. I love the rich holiday feasts. I love giving gifts (a little too much I'm afraid). Most of all, I love having a whole month to celebrate the advent of Christ. My imagination runs wild when I ponder over thoughts of what it must have been like for Joseph and Mary AND for God. I imagine that Joseph and Mary were scared to death and full of anxious expectation as well as excitement and joy. I imagine that God was smiling and brimming with anticipation as He waited for just the right moment to shatter the silence of our world with the cry of a tiny baby. Not just any baby though! This baby was the Savior of the world! With His birth came a great and glorious light. A light to open the eyes of the blind...a light to guide our hearts towards home...a light to overpower the darkness of sin. A great and glorious light!

This Christmas, I was filled with a whole new treasure trove of emotions and sentimental thoughts. I could not avoid asking if this would be our last Christmas as a family. I had to assure myself that it wouldn't. I had to force myself to focus on the here and now in order to not miss capturing new, special memories. I was determined to allow this trial to teach me something new and add to my love of all things "Christmas". All I wanted for Christmas this year was the joy of another day. That is a gift that will never be taken from me. Each day, to wake up and find the joy of another day for as long as another day comes. That was a gift I knew God would give and a gift I was ready to receive!

Before Christmas arrived, we had to make a trip back to Duke. This was Mike's second check-up and MRI at the brain tumor center. I am not quite sure if this one was more or less nerve wracking than the previous trip. The first one had its own reasons for creating anxiety, but so did this trip. The first MRI was clean, but would this one be? To top it off, I was not going with Mike. His mom and dad had been wanting to travel to Duke with him, so we decided this would be a good time for them to go. I was glad they were able to go, but I was also struggling with the decision. Mike was feeling very confident that the MRI would be clean. I was hoping and praying that his confidence was coming from the Holy Spirit's confirmation that this would be the case. We'll see!

## Christmas Came Early.....

Christmas came early for our family this year!!!! Our Christmas gift...another "beautiful" MRI!!!! Thank you Jesus for the gift of good news...the gift of good health...the gift of peace!

Mike's platelets were 56, which is the lowest they have dipped. So...he will have his blood tested on Friday. If they dip down to 50, they will adjust the dosage of his medications (otherwise, this trend will continue to worsen). If he is not able to start chemo this coming Monday, the doctor said he could wait until Dec. 27. That means that we can head to Texas on the 17th and not have to get back until the 27th. Mike will be feeling great for the trip, too - another answer to prayer! We are really looking forward to seeing my family this year and celebrating Christmas with them (it has been close to 10 years since we have been with my family for Christmas). Plus, we would be back and possibly be able to spend some time with Mike's family as well...a win-win!

God is so gracious to do exceedingly and abundantly more than we could ever ask or imagine (Eph 3:20)...both in us and for us!!!! I believe that with all my heart! That is God's ultimate desire...to do in us and for us what He, and only He, could possibly do! It is in those moments that the world can witness His glory, grace, power, love, and more. It is not only for us...it is for His glory! Oh how I want to always have the heart and mindset to believe these truths and be looking for God's hand at work in my life – even in the mundane, day-to-day busyness of life!

Thank you all for your constant and faithful outpouring of love, support, and encouragement! What a beautiful thing it has been to be a part of such a glorious expression of God's love!

With eyes wide open...

## *A Sweet Christmas Memory!!!!!*

I am finding some much needed time to be still! Waiting on Mallory as she practices for the Living Christmas Tree program, I am listening to the sweet sounds and melodies that tell the story of the greatest miracle ever...God, coming to earth as a baby to shatter the darkness and save the world! I am taken back to memories of my first Christmas with Christ in my heart. We were at a hanging of the greens ceremony at our church in Indiana where Mike and I came to know Christ as our Savior. The story of Christmas came to life that night in my heart like never before. After the presentation and hanging of the greens, the congregation gathered on the front steps of the church, and as the snow fell, we sang Silent Night. I cried then, and I cry now thinking about that night when my heart fully understood the gift of Jesus and the magnitude of His birth.

I am guessing this Christmas will hold many special memories for our family. But shouldn't they all? Unfortunately, it has become far too easy to get caught in the hustle and bustle of the season and miss the glory of Christmas. It takes such effort not to get sucked into the commercial side of things.

Mike and I both want to wish you a Merry Christmas. We pray that the true joy of Christmas floods your heart and fills your homes! We pray that you will be as equally blessed as we are and that you will receive a special Christmas miracle. Can't we all use a miracle in some way!?!?!?!?!?! Know that we pray for you all. We know some of the needs you face, but God knows them all...and we are lifting you up and asking God to supply your every need and reveal Himself to you in a way that leaves you forever changed!

Merry Christmas!

# *Glory In The Highest...*

Several years ago, almost to this very day, I faced one of the loneliest most painful experiences of my life...saying good-bye to my best friend. We had grown up together, played sports together, dated together, comforted each other's broken hearts, stood up for each other on our wedding day, celebrated the births of our children together. We were more like sisters than friends! Kindred spirits! Although we spent many years separated by thousands of miles, our hearts were always close! When Karen died, I traveled home to attend her funeral. I woke up early that morning, kissed my kids' cheeks as they lay sleeping all snuggled up in their beds, hugged Mike, and headed to the airport. I remember sitting in the airport parking lot and sobbing. I prayed and asked Jesus to remind me that I was not alone on this journey. I begged Him to continually remind me of that truth and to help me feel Him by my side over the next couple of days.

On the leg from Knoxville to Cincinnati, I ready Psalm 119 - one of my favorite passages in scripture, and I also read the story of Jesus birth. As we were on our final approach, I looked out my window and saw the most glorious sights I have ever seen. The darkness of the world below and the heavens above were separated by a brilliant band of orange and in the still dark morning sky...a star...one star...shining so brightly! The Bright and Morning Star was with me!

As I traveled back home to Knoxville, I sat and wrote in my journal and filled page after page recording the many ways God had revealed Himself to me over the past few days. Again, as we made our final approach into Knoxville, I looked out the window. It was cloudy and I was unable to see the city lights below. But then, I looked up. My eyes could not believe the sight I saw. As we were flying through the night sky, a meteor shower was taking place. It was as if we were literally in the mesosphere among the blazing meteors. Thousands of shooting stars lit up the darkness. I will never forget that moment. Nothing I have seen since has compared to its magnificence! Psalm 8:1-4 came to life in my heart and in my mind...

*"LORD, our Lord,*
*how majestic is your name in all the earth!*
*You have set your glory*
*in the heavens.*
*Through the praise of children and infants*
*you have established a stronghold against your enemies,*
*to silence the foe and the avenger.*
*When I consider your heavens,*
*the work of your fingers,*
*the moon and the stars,*
*which you have set in place,*
*what is mankind that you are mindful of them,*
*human beings that you care for them?"*

His glory is TRULY more than our minds can imagine. Still, we catch glimpses of it here on this earth if the eyes of our hearts are open to see. Glory in the highest! So worthy of our praise! So worthy of our attention and our worship! SO worthy! Who are WE that He is mindful of us...yet this God who created such beauty and magnificence longs to know us so intimately! Mind boggling, isn't it?

I am so thankful that I have those memories tucked so tightly into my heart! Occasionally, like sorting through a box of heirlooms, I am taken back in time to moments like these when I saw with clarity the very heart of God...so tender...so loving...so intimate...so real!

This weekend at our Living Christmas Tree program, we sang Chris Tomlin's beautiful song *Glory in the Highest*[11]. If you've not heard it, I encourage you to take a moment to do so and let the words flood your heart keeping in mind the season we are about to celebrate...the season of light (Jesus) coming to this dark world to conquer sin and death so that someday, we can all sing "glory in the highest" in the very presence of our King!

Mike and I both feel so blessed this year. We are excited to celebrate Christmas with both our families...something we have not

138

been able to do in many years. Mike's platelets were only up to 64 on Friday, so he is definitely not starting chemo this week. He will wait until the 27th which enables him to enjoy Christmas feeling strong! That is a gift! May the magnificence of His glory fill your heart this Christmas and may you be touched in a special way by the joy of Christmas...the celebration of Jesus' birth...God WITH US...Emmanuel!

Lord, I'm amazed by You!

## *For Unto Us...*

It is Christmas Eve! Wow...Where has this year gone? SO much has happened...so much has changed...so much has been given. But the greatest gift of all was given over 2000 years ago. For unto us a child was given...Wonderful Counselor, Ever Lasting Father, Prince of Peace. The gift of love...hope...life...the gift of Jesus...Emmanuel...God WITH us! No longer separated from our Maker...no longer trapped in darkness. The light has come...In the City of David...our Savior was born. For those who choose to seek Him and follow Him, there is life...real life...eternal life. Hope, in the form of a tiny baby, came on a quiet night in Bethlehem. There were many distractions...many things to worry about...many things that seemed more significant. Not much has changed since then when it comes to our world. Still today...many distractions...many things to worry about...many things seeming more significant than pausing to notice God with us.

As Mike and the kids and I celebrate Christmas this year there are many distractions...many things to worry about...many things that seem significant...but none more worthy of our attention or more significant than the celebration of Jesus' birth. In some ways, our circumstances have helped to remove distractions, eliminate worry, and minimize the significance of many things we once saw as important. I won't lie...there are moments when I turn and face the monster of fear and worry as the reality of our circumstances come to the forefront of my mind. However, the Holy Spirit quickly brings to mind Truth that jumps into my hand like a swift and powerful sword, enabling me to defeat that monster! And then...there is peace...joy...and hope!

As I write this journal entry, I am praying for all who will read it. I am praying that the peace that Jesus brought to this world will flood your hearts and rule your life in the coming year. I am praying that Jesus lives in you...that you have opened His gift of salvation and that you are experiencing the blessings of a relationship with the God who created you and loves you with a perfect, everlasting love. There is no greater gift!!!!! His perfect love is the answer to everything!

We have had a wonderful week here in Texas with my family. It has been a long time coming! Mike has had a great week. He has felt strong. He had his platelets tested on Monday and they were at 143. He will start chemo on Monday. We will head back to Knoxville on Saturday. Please pray for safe travels. According to the weather report, they are expecting snow from Alabama north. This has already been an "eventful" trip, so please pray that the excitement is over and that we make it home with no problems. In case you have not heard, Davis had a stomach bug and then, later in the week, had to have a spot on his thigh lanced and tested for staph. Needless to say, that is enough excitement for us!

## *An Unexpected Development...*

Just wanted to update everyone on Mike's treatment schedule. He went in Monday to have his routine blood test before starting chemo. Turns out, the doctor is concerned about his white blood cell and hemoglobin counts and did not allow him to start chemo. We were shocked. We have only had to be concerned about platelets up to this point. With all the sickness that goes on this time of year, the doctor said it would be too risky given that Mike would be more susceptible to pneumonia and other illnesses.

Please pray for us to have peace in the midst of this new twist. We are not really sure what obstacles this challenge will bring into the mix. We would not be surprised if Duke ends up adjusting Mike's dosage of chemo, particularly the Topotecan. He is now three weeks behind in his treatment schedule. We also do not know how these delays and blood count issues might jeopardize Mike's involvement in the clinical trial at Duke (if at all?). Just when we are resting peacefully in God's grace, it is time to take our faith to a new level. But...we know that His grace is always sufficient and His power is made perfect in our weakness...so that gives us great hope!

# Coincidence...I Think NOT!!!!

He's an on time God! Mike talked to Duke and they cleared him to start chemo. They were not concerned about his white counts. Come to find out, it is actually a good thing that Mike did not start treatment yesterday because his second chemo, that he would have started today, did not get shipped from Duke and would not have arrived on time. OR...did God delay the shipment because Mike did not start his first chemo yesterday? Either way, we thank God for caring about the tiny, intimate details of our life and this journey we are on.

It would be so easy to just move on without taking time to stop and consider a lesson in this circumstance. What have we learned about God...what have we seen Him do...what have we learned about ourselves and our faith in Him? Before we even talked to Duke, I had told Mike that I never want to go back to where I was before we started on this journey in terms of my faith and trust in God. I don't want to become too accustomed to this feeling of peace that when the next challenge or obstacle comes I forget that God is a mountain mover. Instead, I want my response to be motivated by all that I have learned and experienced these past few months.

God is in control...He hears our prayers...He has a plan and His will is perfect. Trusting that and believing that with all my heart has given me such a firm confidence that God sees it all and from a much greater perspective than we do. As it is written in Psalm 121:1-8...

141

*"I lift up my eyes to the mountains—*
*where does my help come from?*
*My help comes from the LORD,*
*the Maker of heaven and earth.*
*He will not let your foot slip—*
*he who watches over you will not slumber;*
*indeed, he who watches over Israel*
*will neither slumber nor sleep.*
*The LORD watches over you—*
*the LORD is your shade at your right hand;*
*the sun will not harm you by day,*
*nor the moon by night.*
*The LORD will keep you from all harm—*
*he will watch over your life;*
*the LORD will watch over your coming and going*
*both now and forevermore."*

This great truth dwells in my heart and is a shield around my mind when the darts of doubts, confusion, and fear come flying at me! Thank you Lord for giving us your armor to protect us and equip us for the battles we face (Ephesians 6).

Rejoice with us and share with others the glory of our King!

## What A Difference A Day Makes!!!

It has been a crazy day! Mike woke up this morning feeling terrible. Yesterday, he seemed a bit fuzzy and slightly disoriented. As the day went on, I just did not have a good feeling. Mike started complaining about a headache so I called the doctor's office at Thompson. They wanted to see Mike. We went in and they ordered an MRI to check for a brain bleed and/or swelling. Talk about sitting on pins & needles! The MRI was clean...PRAISE THE LORD!!!!! While Dr. McCachren was talking to us about the MRI results, Mike started to get sick again. Dr. McCachren suggested he spend the night in the hospital and receive IV fluids. We agreed! Mike has not been able to keep anything down all day and I was worried about dehydration. I stayed with Mike until about 10:30pm. He was feeling a bit better and had managed to keep down crackers and sprite. He took a round of chemo just before I left so we'll see how long that lasts.

Dr. McCachren said he wasn't quite sure what was going on, but thought that maybe Mike had just picked up a bug and the symptoms were magnified due to chemo. That is what we are hoping for. There are some other possibilities that are more serious (related to treatment), but we both think it is a bug. If Mike manages to keep fluids down, he will come home tomorrow. Off to bed...I'm wiped out!

Resting in His grace...

## We're Home!!!!!

Praise the Lord...we are home! Mike stopped throwing up last night around 7:00. He was able to take his chemo last night and keep it down and has eaten well today. The doctor increased his anti-nausea meds and gave him steroids in his IV. That seems to have helped. Mike must have been pretty dehydrated. They pumped lots of fluids in and not much was coming out (if ya know what I mean).

He is feeling much better tonight and glad to be home. The doctor is still unable to determine exactly what was happening. We really think it was a bug and on top of chemo...it was just a bad combination. Happy New Year, everyone. Be safe and here's to a year filled with God's blessings and grace!

## He Is Making All Things New...

Change...people tend to either love it or hate it. Some people don't necessarily love it, but they tolerate it. I am learning to appreciate change! In my quiet time today, I was reading about how God uses change and how essential change is to growth. Do I come to God with a teachable spirit, anticipating the changes He will bring that are necessary for transformation? After all, God is all about transformation! He desires to make all things new...to transform what has been broken and marred by sin into the beautiful creation He set out to design. Why is it that we resist change? Why is it that our response to change is often one of dread and frustration? Is it because we have become content and accustomed to living life in our own power and able to accomplish our daily tasks without the help and power of God?

Do I see change as an opportunity to be transformed? Do I come to God each day with positive, excited expectations or with dread and uncertainty because I do not know what the day or my future holds? Can I trust Him in the dark as much as I do when I seem to be walking in the light of day when things make sense and my path is clear? I don't know about you, but I want to learn to appreciate and benefit from change. Growth requires change! I want to walk through the journey of Mike's cancer and come out on the other end, regardless of what it looks like, having a greater love for and trust in God.

Life IS going to change! We cannot avoid change...period! So...the question is...how are we going to respond to change? What will be the outcome and result of the changes we experience? Whether we experience the change as positive or negative, God sees it as perfect and a necessary tool in accomplishing His perfect will for our lives. I am so glad I can trust God...no matter what! Aren't you? Psalm 105:5 tells us to *remember* the wonders He has done. What a great way to influence our perspective on the changes that lie ahead...to *remember* God's goodness and faithfulness in the past!

Mike is starting to rebound from his last round of chemo. This was a rough one. He is also having some trouble with his back. His spirits are good though. He just keeps pluggin' along! We are so thankful for how well he is doing. Things could be so much worse and we are always aware of that fact. If you did not know what he is going through, you'd say he is the picture of health. We thank God for that! The next few months will be a challenge for him. We realized last week that he is going to have to stay close to home and away from people for a while since his blood counts are low compared to normal. Please pray that he will not feel too isolated. We appreciate the cards, phone calls, e-mails, text, etc. That helps him feel more connected.

Counting our blessings...

# *Refining Fire...*

Hello, friends. Just wanted to give you all a quick update on Mike. He is feeling strong right now! His back is bothering him a bit, but, for the most part, he is feeling good. His platelets were at 59 Monday and his white blood cell count was down a bit. So...the trend continues! Most likely, he will start his next round of chemo on January 31, assuming his blood counts go back up. Pray that we continue to have peace and trust God's plan completely...even when our emotions try to convince us not to!

Last weekend, our student ministry participated in a weekend of discipleship called Merge. During worship, we sang a song and the lyrics reminded me of the benefits, purpose, and blessings that come from God's refining fire. I thought about how much I love sitting by an open fire. At first, the fire is somewhat aggressive and causes me to back away from its overwhelming heat. Then, as time goes by, the fire settles down and becomes a warm, comforting place to be and the beautiful, mesmerizing glow of the coals captures my attention and gaze with a calming, comforting effect.

Our God is a consuming fire! He often brings fire into our lives to burn away chaff or anything that He considers an impurity in our lives. This is often a painful, frightening process, but the results are beautiful. I think of Jeremy Camp's song *Empty Me*[12]...holy fire...burn away...my desire for anything that is not of you but is of me...I want more of you and less of me...empty me! As I sat last night and looked through a scrapbook made for us by dear friends, I couldn't help but feel a warm glow in my heart. This "fire" was a barn burner at first. In the beginning, it felt so consuming and destructive...but now...we are enjoying the warm, inviting glow of His glory and love.

Is there a fire raging in your life right now? Hang on! Trust and allow God to use it to purify your life and bring forth the beauty that He desires. When Shadrach, Meshach and Abednego were in the fiery furnace the only thing that burned up were the cords that bound them. They came out of the fire and did not even smell like smoke (Daniel 3). God's holy fire always has a purpose...to free us from what binds us...to refine our hearts...to bring to the surface anything that makes us impure...so that these impurities can be removed and so others can look at us and see His reflection.

Presenting my life as a burnt offering is so difficult! I don't like pain...I don't like the searing heat of the fire...but I love the warm, gentle glow once the fire dies down! Ooooops...my quick update turned into more than I had expected! But I can't help singing praises to Him!

Enjoying the glow...

## Our Every Need...

Mike had his blood counts checked again today and they continued to drop (platelets, whites, & reds). The trend continues and continues to worsen each month. Platelets were down to 44 today. Duke had mentioned that if they drop below 50, they will have to reduce Mike's dosage of Topotecan (chemo). These drops also extend the time between treatment rounds as his body/counts takes longer and longer to rebound.  So...two concerns here...having to reduce chemo dosage and longer periods of time between treatments. It is what it is...and although we obviously respond with concern, we have peace that God is in control and hears and answers our prayers according to His perfect will. He knows every intricate detail of Mike's body and knows what he needs before we or the doctors do.  Thank you for your continued prayers and support!

### Our Every need...

You see us each and every day
You know our thoughts
You know our needs

Your kingdom is vast
Your storehouse complete
Treasures in heaven unseen

Pouring forth from your heart
You withhold nothing
As a Father cares for His child

Though we don't often know
What our hearts are longing for
You've thought of every possible need

We are never without
Your love and your grace
Jesus...
You satisfy our every need!

Trusting the Giver of our every need...

## Holding Pattern...

Mike had his blood checked on Monday. His platelets were up to 84 and his whites and reds were up a bit but still low. He is headed in the right direction! We are hoping that he will start chemo on Monday...assuming counts continue to rise. We have not heard for sure what Duke will do concerning the dose of chemo, but we are pretty confident that the Topotecan will be reduced.

We have learned, finally, not to expect or predict the certainty of our circumstances through all this. However, that does not mean that everything in life is unpredictable or uncertain! God is the same yesterday, today, and tomorrow...still faithful...still true...still sovereign...still with us...still for us...still sees us...still loves us...still our healer...still our Savior...still God!

I love knowing, even in the midst of a "holding pattern", that God is still at work! His work never ceases!!!! Even when we seem to be going nowhere...even when our circumstances seem to be unchanging...even when we seem stuck...God is still moving and working!!!!! What a great treasure to know that God is alive and always working to complete the work He has begun. Sometimes that work just involves stillness...times to camp out and rest in His glory. Eventually...His "cloud or pillar of fire" will begin to move in a new direction and we will pack up our camp and follow Him. Unfortunately, sometimes we want to tell God where we want to camp out...what comforts we expect...what pleasures we hope to find...as if being in His presence is not enough!

To be honest...I am learning to enjoy this season of camping out with the Lord. He has placed an enormous hedge of protection around us, and even though our enemy is constantly trying to break through that hedge, He continues to fight for us and keeps us safe within the refuge of His wings. I will also be honest and say that, at times, it "feels" like the enemy is about to overcome, but when we cry out to the Lord, calling on His name, He is always there and we are always safe in His eternal love. We are eternally His! This world is not our home! In the end...regardless of the battles here on earth...WE WIN!

**Where You are...**

Your cloud and pillar
My heart long's to follow

Your presence and glory
My heart's greatest desire

But is that enough
When my flesh wants more

Will I notice when You move
Will I grow too content

Will I fall asleep
In the comforts of this world


What a frightening thought
To awaken in the dark

And find that I've missed your call

So I'll fix my eyes on You, Lord
Anchor my heart to Yours

I am waiting on you, Lord
I will not move
I will rest in the place where you are

Holding on during the holding patterns...

149

## Number 6...

If all goes well, Mike will reach the half way milestone for chemo tomorrow!!!!! If his blood counts are up, he should have an Avastin treatment and start the next round of chemo...NUMBER 6!!!!

Please, please, please continue to pray. Mike has actually reached one of the most critical points in treatment. Pray earnestly! It is incredibly important that he continue to have clean MRI's. This point in treatment is often a period when things start to "change" and tumor growth can become evident. We are hopeful that will not be the case for Mike and that he will continue to be cancer free for the remainder of treatment...and the remainder of his life!!!!! But we also know the reality of his circumstances and the power of prayer in terms of the outcome. We need and appreciate your prayers more than words can express. Pray for God's perfect will to be done. Pray for healing. Pray for our journey to be one that draws the eyes of others to the glorious cross and our wonderful Savior and loving Father. Our next trip to Duke will probably be mid to late February. We will update you tomorrow and let you know if he was able to start chemo and if Duke decided to reduce the dosage of his chemo.

## So Far, So Good...

Our family has been hit by the stomach bug! So far, Mike has managed to avoid Mallory's virus. Praise the Lord!!! His Topotecan dosage was reduced as expected. Last night was his first night of this round to take both chemos. He woke up a bit queasy. Hopefully his anti-nausea meds nipped it in the bud.

I continue to be amazed by Mike's perseverance, his selflessness, and his overall attitude. Seriously...amazed!!!! I cannot even imagine what shape I would be in physically, emotionally, and psychologically if I were in his shoes. I know it is the Lord and the strength and hope that come from Mike's walk with Him.

150

I've been singing a song in my head all day long...*You Never Let Go* by Matt Redman[13]. The words are so true and so powerful! They are a beautiful prayer and declaration of faith, hope, and love. I cannot help but think about Mike when I listen to this song. He has remained so focused on eternity throughout this whole ordeal. Not just the destination of his eternity...but the purpose of all of this from the perspective of eternity and how God desires to use his cancer to impact the eternity of others perhaps. Here are the lyrics to the song...

*Even though I walk through the valley*
*Of the shadow of death*
*Your perfect love is casting out fear*

*And even when I'm caught in the middle*
*Of the storms of this life*
*I won't turn back, I know You are near*

*And I will fear no evil*
*For my God is with me*
*And if my God is with me*
*Whom then shall I fear?*
*Whom then shall I fear?*

*Oh no, You never let go*
*Through the calm and through the storm*
*Oh no, You never let go*
*In every high and every low*
*Oh no, You never let go*
*Lord, You never let go of me*

*And I can see a light that is coming*
*For the heart that holds on*
*A glorious light beyond all compare*

*And there will be an end to these troubles*
*But until that day comes*
*We'll live to know You here on the earth*

*And I will fear no evil*
*For my God is with me*
*And if my God is with me*
*Whom then shall I fear?*
*Whom then shall I fear?*

*Oh no, You never let go*
*Through the calm and through the storm*
*Oh no, You never let go*
*In every high and every low*
*Oh no, You never let go*
*Lord, You never let go of me*

*You keep on loving*
*And You never let go*

(and this reminds me most of Mike)
***Yes, I can see a light that is coming***
***For the heart that holds on***
***And there will be an end to these troubles***
***But until that day comes***
***Still I will praise You, still I will praise You***

(he just keeps on praisin' God!!!!!!)

   What a comfort to know that God just keeps hangin' on! What a blessing that His perfect love truly casts out all fears when it is invited to come and take over our hearts and our lives. What a mystery that even in the midst of pain, suffering, and any sort of trial...we can still praise Him because of the HOPE that is in our hearts and our confidence in the

Light that will soon come!!!! One day...we will see Him face to face and He will wipe away every tear...there will be no more suffering, no more pain, no more cancer! What a great and glorious day that will be. We were never meant to be content and comfortable in this world. He has placed a longing for eternity in our hearts...we are strangers in this world. We are just passin' through!

*"For God, who said, 'Let light shine out of darkness,' made his light shine in our hearts to give us the light of the knowledge of God's glory displayed in the face of Christ."* II Cor. 4:6

Seeking that beautiful face...

## Whew...What A Week...

The title of this entry says it all, but hey, it is 4am and I am wide awake so I think I'll journal a bit. Mallory ended up missing the entire week of school. We still do not know exactly what she had. The doctor tested her for strep, the flu (twice), mono, and a urinary tract infection. So far, the tests were all negative. We are waiting for some blood work to come back Monday. She is feeling MUCH better, so maybe it was a virus that has run its course.

Mike managed to stay healthy this week. All in all, it has not been too rough of a round of chemo. He has been nauseated, but his "happy" cream, Zofran, and steroids seem to have taken the edge off. Last night was his last dose for this round so it's up hill from here...as far as we know!

Mike's next appointment at Duke will be Feb. 22 & 23. He will have an MRI, a base line PET scan, and see the doctor. The PET will show much more than an MRI. It will show any metabolic activity of cancer cells. This will give them something to compare to at the end of the clinical trial and will help them determine Mike's treatment needs after the clinical trial, IF ANY!

Davis and I drove to Chattanooga yesterday to visit friends. We had a great time. I was asked what I have learned over the past 10 months (WOW! it has almost been a year...crazy), and something new came to mind. I have such a peace and lack of worry and dread. I have never been a serious worrier, but I have been one to get uptight and anxious when I have had to face a challenge or hardship. God helped me see that, for me, worry and anxiousness has not so much been due to a lack of trust in Him, but an issue of selfishness in my heart...an anxiousness or dread that has come from the fact that I do not WANT to face struggles and hardships....I do not want to suffer or struggle. Thank you, Lord, for opening my eyes to see that!!! It was a blind spot. Great peace comes from surrendering to the call of Christ to take up our cross and follow Him...even into the realm of great suffering and pain. These are places where His grace is often most evident and highly concentrated!!!!

When we accept suffering and pain, we step into a new place of intimacy with our Savior. It is as if we are on a little retreat with Him in a place that can be accessed no other way...the doorway to this place IS suffering. Unfortunately, it takes a great deal of courage and willingness to go there. We have an open invitation to come. Yes...we still suffer...but there is a peace and a blessing in the suffering when we walk through the doorway of **accepting** our suffering and **thanking** God for an opportunity to experience His grace and love THROUGH suffering. Am I even making sense? I hope so...I want so badly to share this joy and gift with you.

*"My comfort in my suffering is this: Your promise preserves my life."*
Psalm 119:50

*"But those who suffer he delivers in their suffering; he speaks to them in their affliction."* Job 36:15 **(notice how this verse says "in" not "from")**

*"...And we boast in the hope of the glory of God. Not only so, but we also glory in our sufferings, because we know that suffering produces*

154

*perseverance; perseverance, character; and character, hope. And hope does not put us to shame, because God's love has been poured out into our hearts through the Holy Spirit, who has been given to us."* Romans 5:2-5

### Will I hurt for you?

Will I go to places others won't go
Will I find joy in pain and sorrow

Will I lay down my life
Take up my cross
Follow you into the dark

Will I forsake all
Will I give you my life
Will I glory in life's pain and trials

Or will I refuse
To know your great love
and the power of your grace through pain
Lord, open my eyes
to my selfish desires
Have you not given everything for me

What more could I want
What more could I find
Than the life that your blood purchased for me

This life cost you greatly, Lord
Yet you counted it a joy
To lay down your life at Calvary

Should I be so selfish, Lord
Should I only accept the good
Will I not accept pain as you did

For it is pain that brings healing
It is pain that brings life
It is pain that brings my heart to yours

Will I settle for ease
Will I demand more from you
Or, Lord, will I hurt for you

Anxiousness, worry, and dread....maybe they are not just symptoms of a lack of faith and trust in God...maybe they are the result of our selfish desire to avoid pain and the unknown!

# Good Report Today...

Mike went to his weekly appointment today to have his blood checked. His platelets were 173 and his whites and red blood counts were back up in the normal range....thank you, Lord!!!! His platelet count this week is higher in comparison to previous months just one week after chemo. This is probably due to the reduction in the dosage of Topotecan. We are hopeful that his platelets won't bottom out as low as they have and that he will be able to start his next round of chemo on time after his trip to Duke next week.

Please join us in praying for this trip to Duke. As I mentioned before, Mike will have a PET scan. This is different from an MRI. They inject a radioactive sugar serum into him and then do the scan. The PET scan will pick up on any metabolic activity of minute cancer cells...they will literally light up due to the sugar...tumors love sugar! The PET scan will pick up on cells that are too small for an MRI to detect. We had thought they would only do a PET scan at the end of treatment, but apparently, Dr. V likes to do one after 6 rounds of chemo to compare to the PET scan at the end of the trial. This will enable them to make decisions concerning Mike's treatment plan following the clinical trial.

Needless to say...this will be a big day and a nerve racking day! The PET scan will be done early in the morning on Feb 23rd.

Hanging on...

# *Your Story...*

God provided our greatest need at Calvary when He allowed His Son to die for our sins, yet we often doubt that God can or will meet our everyday needs. The truth is...He can and will do exceedingly and abundantly more than we could ever ask or imagine each and every day of our lives. Unfortunately, we can often miss seeing what He is doing because His ways don't exactly match up with our ways or how we would like our answered prayers to look. Do you see God working in your life right now or is your vision of His work in your life blurred by your own selfish desires, fears, of doubt? Spend some time praying and praising God for His provision. If need be, open your heart and eyes to the exceeding, abundant ways God is working in your life today.

Chapter Ten

# *Half Way...*

*"Humble yourselves therefore under the mighty hand of God, so that He may exalt you in due time, casting all your care upon Him, because He cares about you." 1 Peter 5:6-7 HCSB*

Praise God! Mike made it through 6 rounds of treatment. In some ways, this has been the longest year of my life and, at the same time, it has been the shortest year of my life. Some days and weeks seem to last an eternity and others fly by in the blink of an eye. I believe that is just the grace of God knowing when we needed life to slow down and when we needed it to speed up and hurry on by.

With each round of treatment that Mike was able to complete there was both celebration and anxiousness. We were thankful that he was moving closer to the end of his 12 treatments, but we also knew that this is often the point at which a large majority of GBM patients find out that residual cancer cells have been able to grow in spite of the chemo and other drugs. It was a constant struggle to remain focused on what we know to be true rather than False Evidence Appearing Real (FEAR). However, when we fixed our eyes on Jesus and allowed Him to renew our minds, we were filled with unexplainable peace...a peace that could only come from the true Source of peace...our Savior and loving Father.

Once again, Mike was traveling to Duke with his parents and I was staying home. While Mike was at his last Duke visit and I was home, we realized how stressful it was on the kids when both of us traveled to Duke. We also decided that me being home was best for the kids and helps eliminate a large amount of their stress and anxiety. However, we made this decision BEFORE we realized Mike would be having a PET scan during this visit. Me being there would not change the results and it probably would not reduce my level of anxiety, but I sure was torn!

So...as the day approached, I was determined to look my enemy, fear, in the eyes and declare the sovereignty of my King and my unshakable faith in Him! So long fear...

# Looking Fear In The Eyes...

Today has been a difficult day. As I sat in church, I began to feel anxious and overwhelmed by emotions. As I thought about the week ahead, I felt the urge to pray, and that is when the anxiousness began. *O.K., Lord...your Word says be anxious for nothing...but through prayer and supplication with thanksgiving I can present my requests to you and experience the peace that surpasses all understanding...so why am I anxious? I know it is not because you refuse to give me Your peace, so what am I holding on to? What is in my heart and mind that is keeping me from experiencing your peace?*

I realized that I was struggling to ask the Lord for what I wanted...complete and total healing for Mike. Why is it so difficult sometimes for me to pray for healing? I know that God can and will heal Mike, but I also know that His will may not include Mike's total healing. So...if I don't ask, I won't be disappointed, right? But God does not want our cautious prayers! He wants us to acknowledge our complete and total trust in Him...our belief that He can indeed heal...that He will heal...that He does heal. He wants us to acknowledge our willingness to surrender to and accept His will even if it does not match up to our desired outcome.

I also realized that praying for Mike's healing also puts me in a very vulnerable place. When I pray for healing, I am forced to look fear in the eyes and feel the emotions that are often buried beneath my strong exterior. Thankfully, God is always there to strengthen me in my time of weakness! He has yet to allow me to be overtaken by my enemy, fear!

So...as we head into a very important week...I am feeling strong! I have looked fear in the eyes and survived. We are ready to see what the Lord has in store. We are asking for healing, trusting that He can heal, and accepting His good pleasing and perfect will. This has been an exhausting wrestling match!

His grace is sufficient, and His power is made perfect in our weakness! So...I am not afraid to boast in my weakness...because it is then that the power of Christ rests on me and guards my heart (2 Cor. 12:9). When I am weak...He is strong!

**So long fear...**

So long fear
You're not welcome here
There is no room for you in my heart

Your goal is despair
Your desire to destroy
You are selfish, destructive and cruel

So long fear
I refuse to be yours
I am covered by His grace and His love

My King will ride in
He'll conquer your lies
He will shower my heart with His peace

The victory is mine
You will not win!
I will not become your prey
So long fear
His love has arrived
Casting you out once again!

Ready for the results...

# How Deep The Father's Love...

Today has been one of those days when I have just felt overwhelmed by God's love. He is calming my anxious heart and He is singing songs of peace over me as I wait and wish I were with Mike at Duke. I am almost weepy. There are tears of joy and gratitude ready to break through at any moment. I cannot stop singing *How Deep The Father's Love*[14] in my head and in my heart.

*How deep the Father's love for us*
*How vast beyond all measure*
*That He would give His only Son*
*To make a wretch His treasure*

*How great the pain of searing loss*
*The Father turns His face away*
*As wounds that mar the chosen One*
*Bring many sons to glory*

*Behold the man upon the cross*
*My sins upon His shoulders*
*Ashamed I hear my mocking voice*
*Cry our among the scoffers*

*It was my sin that held Him there*
*Until it was accomplished*
*His dying breath has brought me life*
*I know that it is finished*

163

*I will not boast in anything*
*No gifts, no powers, no wisdom*
*But I will boast in Jesus Christ*
*His death and resurrection*


*Why should I gain from His reward*
*I cannot give an answer*
*But this I know with all my heart*
*His wounds have paid my ransom*


What a beautiful song...what powerful words! We gain so much from His reward! There is no reasonable explanation that can explain or make sense of why God would choose to bless us after our sin sent His Son to the cross. But, then again, that is what grace is all about...God's unexplainable love and favor for His creation.

Thank you all for your love and prayers today and tomorrow. I cannot wait to share the good news that I am anxiously waiting to hear! As a friend pointed out today...what a sight it would be to see into the spiritual realm as all those prayers surrounded Mike's car, surrounded him in the MRI machine, surrounded him in the PET scan machine, and surrounds our family during this stressful time of waiting. Thank you for each and every prayer that has hemmed us in.

To God be the glory!

## Breathing Again...

Well...we can breathe again for two more months. And this time...we are taking in a huge breath and letting out an enormous sigh of relief. Both the MRI and PET scan came back clean!!!! Praise the only One who is worthy of our praise!

The PET scan was completely dark meaning nothing lit up indicating metabolic activity of residual cancer cells. This is such good news. This news brings such confidence and hope that God is bringing about complete and total healing in Mike. He still has a long way to go, but we are thanking God and giving Him all the praise and glory for this report. This is truly miraculous! A GBM diagnosis is often considered a death sentence and, for most patients, it is only a matter of time rather than "if". So...as you can imagine, we are just completely and utterly overwhelmed by God's grace and provision.

Dr. V explained to Mike that 80% of the clinical trial participants have a clean PET scan after 6 months where as only around 5% of patients have a clean PET scan after 6 months of treatment with standard protocol. Needless to say, God has blessed Mike with the opportunity to participate in this clinical trial. This research is no doubt changing the odds for GBM patients.

One area of concern is Mike's platelet counts. Today they were at 48. This is not good and we had hoped it would not dip down that low after the reduction in Topotecan. Dr. V told Mike that he will no longer be able to participate in the clinical trial if they have to reduce the Topotecan dosage again. If his platelets drop down to 25, he will have to have a transfusion and will be eliminated from the trial. If that is the case, Dr. V said he is almost certain that insurance will approve for Mike to continue receiving Avastin along with Temodar. We don't even want to have to find out if that is the case!

What a great and mighty God we have! He moves mountains and He calms the seas! When I consider all that He has done for my family, I am completely overwhelmed!

O Lord my God,
When I in awesome wonder
Consider all
The works Thy Hand hath made,

I see the stars,
I hear the mighty thunder,
Thy power throughout the universe displayed;

165

When through the woods
And forest glades I wander
I hear the birds
Sing sweetly in the trees;

When I look down
From lofty mountain grandeur
And hear the brook
And feel the gentle breeze;

Then sings my soul,
My Savior God, to Thee,
How great Thou art!
How great Thou art!

Then sings my soul,
My Savior God, to Thee,
How great Thou art!
How great Thou art!

When Christ shall come,
With shouts of acclamation,
And take me home,
What joy shall fill my heart!

Then I shall bow
In humble adoration
And there proclaim,
"My God, how great Thou art!"[15]

What a great and glorious gift that we do not have to wait until
the day that Jesus comes to take us home before we can see the majesty
of God, experience His love, and sing His praises! I, for one, refuse to
allow the rocks to have to cry out...I want to exclaim the glory and

majesty of God to this world. I want others to experience the depths of His love. I want the hearts of others to be touched tenderly by His grace...in a way that brings about hope, healing, peace, comfort, courage, or whatever it is they need.

He IS a great and glorious God regardless of if we proclaim that. Our lack of praise and adoration does not change the fact that He is the King of this universe. Our lack of praise and adoration only robs *us* from experiencing the blessings of His love and grace.

Lift your eyes up to the hills...where does your help come from? Your help comes from the Lord, the maker of heaven and earth! He created you and He watches over you...waiting for you to come to Him...waiting for you to receive His love (Ps. 121).

I've asked God many times these past few days to give me a peace that Mike's PET scan would be clean. Finally, after continuing to pray because there was no peace that this would be the case, God gently reminded me that peace is found in Him rather than the outcome of circumstances. He is our peace...the Prince of Peace...and when He rules our hearts and when our lives are fully surrendered to Him...peace will rule our hearts...regardless of our circumstances or the lack of confidence in what lies ahead.

He will keep those in perfect peace whose minds are steadfast on Him...those who trust HIM (Isaiah 26:3). What a great promise...what a great treasure...what a great God!

The journey continues...

# *Your Story...*

      Waiting on God can be so difficult! Are you waiting on God to do something...to provide something...to deliver you from something? Don't give up! Humble yourself before Him today by confessing and accepting your helplessness! In doing so, you are casting your cares upon His strong shoulders! Trust that, in due time, He will lift you up because He cares so deeply for you and longs to bless you. Trust Him! He will come through for you! Use this time to cry out to God...record your earnest prayer here and then TRUST Him to carry your burdens and lift you up!

An Unfamiliar Path...

Chapter Eleven

# The Path of Peace...

*"Great peace have those who love your law, and nothing can make them stumble." Psalm 119:165*

We seem to have settled into a consistent and comfortable stride. For the most part, life was beginning to feel "normal", or maybe we were growing more and more comfortable with our "new normal." I am not sure if we were growing more accustomed to the reality that nothing was predictable on this unfamiliar path, or if we were somehow discovering some predictable patterns in our monthly cycle of good days and bad days. I guess it doesn't really matter! I was just thankful to be feeling a sense of peace in my heart and in my mind.

God promises that if we come to Him and present our requests, thanking Him ahead of time for how He WILL answer our prayers, He will give us a peace that surpasses all understanding and that He will guard our hearts and minds with this peace (Philippians 4:19). I honestly believe this is something we cannot fully comprehend until we experience it. For most of my life, I have no doubt that peace came not as a result of trusting God, but rather knowing in my heart that I could probably handle just about any circumstance that came my way. One way or another, I could handle things...with God's help of course (wink, wink). In reality, I felt confident in God to some extent because I also felt confident in myself.

Well...I cannot fix this! For the first time in my life, I find myself in a situation that cannot be fixed in my own strength, and I can honestly say...thank you, Lord, for bringing me here and for showing me just how truly faithful and sovereign You are and how completely weak and helpless I am. There is a new sense of freedom in my heart that could have come no other way than by being fully and completely dependent upon You!

It is one thing to speak of having mountain moving faith. It is another thing all together to have to put that faith into action when you stand at the foot of an obstacle the size of Mount Everest, trusting that God can move that mountain or move you to a whole new place of abiding in and trusting Him no matter what! It is in these moments that we learn to cast our cares upon Him, to take up His yoke, to dwell within His shelter, and to soar upon His wings. Easy...NO! Worth it...ABSOLUTELY!

170

*"Those who trust in the LORD are as secure as Mount Zion; they will not be defeated but will endure forever. Just as the mountains surround Jerusalem, so the LORD surrounds his people, both now and forever."*
*Psalm 125:1-2 NLT*

## *Gravity...*

*"Therefore, since we are surrounded by such a huge crowd of witnesses to the life of faith, let us strip off every weight that slows us down, especially the sin that so easily trips us up. And let us run with endurance the race God has set before us. We do this by keeping our eyes on Jesus, the champion who initiates and perfects our faith. Because of the joy awaiting him, he endured the cross, disregarding its shame. Now he is seated in the place of honor beside God's throne. Think of all the hostility he endured from sinful people; then you won't become weary and give up. After all, you have not yet given your lives in your struggle against sin." Hebrew 12:1-4 NLT*

These verses were etched in my heart many years ago. After highlighting the faith of so many amazing people who longed to know and live for God, the author of Hebrews gives us instructions to model their tenacity in living our lives for Christ and encourages us to understand and accept God's discipline/teaching through suffering and other forms of adversity. I had to return to these words this past week in order to overcome an unexpected spiritual struggle.

We received amazing news last week when Mike traveled to Duke, and although I was ecstatic, I quickly settled into a "funk" that I could not shake. I felt weighted down by something, but what...what was stealing my joy and ability to remain on the mountain top of praise and thanksgiving in response to Mike's clean PET scan. I felt a great "weight" that was "slowing me down". Rather than running with endurance, I was feeling weary and heavy laden. Something had

171

distracted my attention and my eyes were not intently fixed on Jesus. So...I fought to turn my attention to Him.

As my gazed returned to Him, I came to realize what was weighing me down. Shortly after feeling the relief and excitement of our good news, I was sucked into a pit. I don't even know what to call this pit. I started going down the list of possible names...was this fear, doubt, dread, disbelief? I could not put my finger on it. My frustration was growing and the weight was crushing my spirit. Lord, what is it that I need to "strip off"?

Well...as always, God was faithful to answer my cry for help. He helped me see that my joy was being outweighed by my dread of the unknown. Yes...we had good news now, but what about the future? After all, the doctors cannot assure us that Mike is cancer free. God began to show me (once again) my need to avoid pain and my tendency to anticipate disappointment. The enemy was taking advantage of this and he was trying to convince me that it was only a matter of time before more bad news came...only a matter of time before the next disappointment arrived. He was tempting me to eat the fruit of despair rather than abiding in God's peace and joy.

In science this week, we were studying about gravity and acceleration due to gravity. Gravity is constantly pulling us down. In order to resist and counteract the pull of gravity, there must be another force to overcome it. Living in this fallen world...living in our flesh...we will always be subject to the pull of sin and we are in constant need of some force to counteract that pull. That force is Jesus...the only force that can overcome the effects of the sin that weighs us down and ensnares us. It is only when we abide in His grace and truth that we can defy the weight and pull of sin and all that hinders us from experiencing His blessings and joy.

I am happy to say that I am back to a place of celebrating God's amazing grace and provision. I refuse to allow Satan to steal my joy and an opportunity to celebrate God's miraculous touch on Mike's life. I don't know what the future holds, but that is OK! I have this day and this moment to enjoy the blessings of His love and care. My flesh may weigh me down, but my spirit can soar weightlessly when I allow God to set me free from all that hinders me...including my flesh! And one glad morning...when this life is over...I will fly away...weightless and unaffected by the pull of sin!

**Weightless...**

My flesh is heavy
A burden I bear
Trapped in this vessel
Longing to be free

Break the chains, Lord
Let my spirit soar
High above the worries
That fill this world

I can't escape pain
There is nowhere to hide
But my pain is relieved
When I rest by Your side

This world is so weighty
Nothing like You designed
In our hope we transcend
The pull of despair

One day we'll be weightless
We will soar and not fall
Set free from gravity...
The pull of sin
The day is coming
A promise you've made
One day we'll be weightless
Forever with You!

# Are You Sitting Down...

Well...if you are, then stand up and shout a praise to the Lord! Mike went in for blood work, fully expecting them to tell him to come back later in the week to re-test and hoping that he would be able to start chemo next week once his platelets were up above 100. Well...God had bigger plans...Mike's platelets were 122 today and he is having an Avastin treatment as I "speak" and will start chemo tonight. Go God! Are you kidding me? His platelets rebounded from the 40's to the 120's in less than a week...only God can get credit for that!!!!! Yet another lesson in understanding the full meaning of His sovereignty, grace, and mercy!

I can't help but think of the words God inspired Paul to write thousands of years ago...words we would all need today to draw from for hope, courage, and assurance...we are pressed but not crushed, persecuted but not abandoned, struck down but not destroyed (II Cor. 4:8,9)! All for the glory of God...to show others His power and might! Like jars of clay God is using this journey to mold us and shape us...filling us with His glorious light so that others might see the glow of His beautiful face. So...I am totally OK with being a cracked pot that provides more opportunities for God's glory to shine! Think about it...if we don't have a few chips, dings, and cracks in our pot (our jar), then God's glory will not be seen as clearly as the glow of His love burns within us. It's OK...embrace your cracked-potness!!! Besides...misery loves company, and I'd like to know there are fellow cracked-pots around me!!!!

I am also reminded of this glorious truth..."*Therefore we do not lose heart. Though outwardly we are wasting away, yet inwardly we are being renewed day by day. For our light and momentary troubles are achieving for us an eternal glory that far outweighs them all. So we fix our eyes not on what is seen, but on what is unseen, since what is seen is temporary, but what is unseen is eternal.*" II Cor 4:16-18

One day, we will have a beautiful, crackless pot when we are finally transformed into the image of Christ...perfect and without any dings or chips caused by this fallen world! And...the glory of that day will outweigh all the challenges of this world...in a moment, our memory of the pain and strife of this world will be gone...faith and hope will no longer be needed...but only love will remain!

Simply amazed...

# *Blessings...*

*"what if your blessings come through rain drops...what if your healing comes through tears...what if a thousand sleepless nights are what it takes to know your near...what if trials of this life are your mercies in disguise...all the while you long that we'd have faith to believe...this pain reminds us that this is not our home...what if the greatest disappointments or the aching of this life is the revealing of a greater thirst this world can't satisfy...and what if trials of this life are your mercies in disguise?"* (from the song, *Blessings,* by Laura Story[16])

I recently received a request from a high school senior who is working on her senior project to answer a question. Her question was this..."Does God truly love you?" Here is my response...

*When I was 26 years old...my eyes and heart were opened to the reality of God's love...Jesus Christ...God's son...sent to pay the price for my sin so that I could live forever with the God who loves me and created me to receive His love. Since that time, I have gained a better understanding of God's perfect, unconditional love. I am amazed by the fact that, even though I could never do anything to deserve God's love, He loves me unconditionally and fully. I do not doubt this love!!!!*

*Even though my family is currently experiencing a dark and dreadful circumstance, I know without a doubt that God loves me. In fact, these circumstances have actually enabled me to experience God's love on a much deeper level. God's love is not expressed through the things He does or will do for us. It is*

175

*expressed by what He HAS already done for us...He died in our place and took the penalty for our sins...that is the ultimate expression of love!*

*The level of comfort and ease of my life does not affect my belief in or ability to trust God's love. His love is an everlasting, unchanging, perfect love! It cannot be diminished by trials, pain, or even death. In fact, death is what brings us, once and for all, into the fullness of God's love by bringing us fully into His presence forever! In the meantime...His perfect love casts out all my fears!*

*"And we know that God causes everything to work together for the good of those who love God and are called according to his purpose for them. For God knew his people in advance, and he chose them to become like his Son, so that his Son would be the firstborn among many brothers and sisters. And having chosen them, he called them to come to him. And having called them, he gave them right standing with himself. And having given them right standing, he gave them his glory.*
*Nothing can separate us from God's love. What shall we say about such wonderful things as these? If God is for us, who can ever be against us? Since he did not spare even his own Son but gave him up for us all, won't he also give us everything else? Who dares accuse us whom God has chosen for his own? No one—for God himself has given us right standing with himself. Who then will condemn us? No one—for Christ Jesus died for us and was raised to life for us, and he is sitting in the place of honor at God's right hand, pleading for us. Can anything ever separate us from Christ's love? Does it mean he no longer loves us if we have trouble or calamity, or are persecuted, or hungry, or destitute, or in danger, or threatened with death? (As the Scriptures say, "For your sake we are killed every day; we are being slaughtered like sheep.")*

*No, despite all these things, overwhelming victory is ours through Christ, who loved us.*

*And I am convinced that nothing can ever separate us from God's love. Neither death nor life, neither angels nor demons, neither our fears for today nor our worries about tomorrow— not even the powers of hell can separate us from God's love. No power in the sky above or in the earth below—indeed, nothing in all creation will ever be able to separate us from the love of God that is revealed in Christ Jesus our Lord." Romans 8:28-39 NLT*

The truth is...God shows His love for us in many ways, and those ways include trials...pain...suffering...and all the difficult circumstances of this life. *What if trials are His mercies in disguise?* What a great question to ponder! Mercy is not getting what we deserve. We truly deserve to suffer the consequences of our sin, but God chooses to give us what we do not deserve...His unconditional love! That is the ultimate blessing...to know and experience and trust the perfect love of God...to believe that NOTHING can separate us from that love...neither death nor life, fears or worries, not even the powers of hell...NO NOTHING can separate us from God's love if we CHOOSE to receive it and place our faith and hope in Christ!

On this long and tiring journey, we continually run smack dab into God's love at each twist and turn! When we are tired...His love carries us. When we are strong...His love is what energizes us. When we are scared...His love calms our hearts. When we are frustrated and weary...His love reassures us and refocuses us. It is in these moments that we realize the thirst of our souls that can only be quenched by His love! The true blessings of God are not ease and comfort, but the ability to soar when life weighs us down.

Praying you are BLESSED today...

# *Blessed...*

Today was blood work day! Mike's reds and whites were down quite a bit and his platelets were at 72. Last month at this time, his platelets were in the low 40's so this is a significant improvement! He needs them to stay above 50 in order to maintain his status in the clinical trial. Praise the Lord for a good count! He will most likely do his next round of chemo the week of April 4. He is postponing the start date by a week so that he can go to Nashville and see the kids compete at the State History Fair.

I've been thinking a lot today about just how much God has blessed us through this journey. We took the kids on a hike Saturday and we talked with them about what they have learned through this whole ordeal and what they have learned about God. It was so sweet to hear them share their hearts and to see how they have grown in their faith and trust in God. Even in moments of darkness, pain, fear, and frustration, we have been blessed! I hesitate sometimes to talk about all the positive, comfortable, "happy" blessings because I know so many people on similar journeys who are fighting to see God's blessings in the midst of circumstances that are far more grave than Mike's. I almost feel selfish sometimes and my heart breaks for others who are not experiencing God's healing touch like Mike or who are struggling physically and emotionally. But...I know that God is working to accomplish His perfect will in their lives, and I know that they are desperate to allow God's will to be done.

Today, I took some time to meditate on the word "blessing". The verses that came to mind are from Genesis when Jacob wrestled with an angel of the Lord and refused to let go until he was blessed. That word in Genesis 32 means to kneel or bend the knee. This certainly was not a pleasant experience for Jacob. He experienced pain and was left with a sore hip and a limp...but...his life was forever changed in a powerful way! In fact, his name was changed from Jacob (deceiver) to Israel (God prevails). In this wrestling match...God prevailed and His will was done...Jacob was forever changed and became the father of the 12 tribes of Israel.

It is during these wrestling matches that God is able to change us in a way that conforms us to His will and image...that is a true blessing...to be so close to God that we are brought to our knees and changed forever. But...will we hang on and refuse to give in and end the wrestling match due to our discomfort, or will we determine to wrestle and hang on until God accomplishes His purpose in our lives...until God blesses us?

So...regardless of the discomfort and displeasure of our circumstances...we are such a blessed family. We have wrestled with God and with our human nature and we have overcome on many occasions and hopefully will continue to overcome the struggles this journey brings. Like Jacob, this has been an opportunity for us to be so close to God that we have seen Him face to face, and yet our lives have been spared. That's what makes this struggle worth the fight and all the pain and frustration!!!!

Blessed...what does the word really mean?

# We Know It Is Chemo Week When...

OK...laughter is good medicine and humor is a wonderful defense mechanism.  So, I thought I'd relieve my angst by posting a top 10 list of how the Hearn family knows it is chemo week at our house....

**#10** - We know it's chemo week when what can go wrong will go wrong

**#9** - We know it's chemo week when all our meals include potato soup or pasta

**#8** - We know it's chemo week when Mike turns a pale shade of green

**#7** - We know it's chemo week when the kitchen counter is lined with prescription bottles

**#6** - We know it's chemo week when Mike is a "little loopy"

**#5** - We know it's chemo week when Mike sleeps more than the cats

**#4** - We know it's chemo week when Mike is not allowed to drive...because he's "loopy"

**#3** - We know it's chemo week when we run out of Sprite and Gatorade

**#2** - We know its chemo week when Lori and the kids have to cook dinner instead of Mike (my least favorite)

And the #1 reason we know it is chemo week...I'll spare you the details!!!!!

Mike was feeling a bit queasy this morning. In fact, I think this is the FIRST morning all year that he has not gotten out of bed to see the kids off to school. This is round 8 so hopefully only 4 more!!!!!!! Now THAT is exciting!!!!!

We are still clinging to the good news from his PET scan and continue to praise God for His grace and goodness! He continues to perform miracles in Mike's life for all the world to see!!!!! We have said from the beginning...when God is involved...statistics mean nothing!!!!! With God...all things are possible!

Have a blessed day...and...laugh...it is good medicine!!!!!

## The Broken Road...

Walking by faith is an arduous task at times. Other times, it seems effortless. Walking this "broken road" has been tough at times, but we have definitely developed endurance that is sure to benefit us as we continue this journey called "life".

As I look back over the past year, my mind's eye conjures up an image of my family scaling Mount Everest...lol! And now, we are on the other side...beginning our descent and ready to head down a new path...hopefully one that has fewer obstacles and hazards that have the potential to cause harm or make us stumble. If not...then we trust that the Lord will continue to guide us and make the rough places smooth.

This may seem odd to some, but I have grown quite accustom to and fond of certain aspects of this detour. For example, a part of me does not want to descend from the mountain and places of complete and utter isolation...places of deep abiding and intimate fellowship. I know that Jesus is always with me, but there have definitely been many "distractions" stripped away over the past year that are likely to sneak back in as our lives return to "normal". I've grown to enjoy this "new normal" in many ways (reminds me of the disciples on the Mount of Transfiguration!) But in reality, life is a constant ebb and flow of new

181

normals. Maybe we will continue to embrace the ebb and flow and remain sensitive to and comfortable with this new appreciation for suffering, surrender to God's perfect will, and desire for Him to be glorified in our lives. I sure hope so! Besides...we must come down from the mountain at some point...faces glowing with His glory...a glow that won't fade like it did for Moses...a glow that will draw others to Him!!!!

Walking by faith is not easy, but it leads to a place of splendor! Like risking and enduring the strenuous climb to a spectacular view atop a mountain...it is worth every step...every stumble...every obstacle that must be overcome...IT IS WORTH IT! But...it is hard none the less!

How sweet that the one year anniversary of the beginning of this journey falls near the celebration of Easter. Our struggles and momentary troubles are sure to pale in comparison to all that our Savior suffered in order that we might rise above the troubles of this world. It is sure to be a sweet time of savoring the joy and peace we have...not because life is easy, but because Jesus has overcome everything in this world that works to break us and keep us from enjoying fellowship with our awesome, loving God.

The Lamb of God was slain and died that we might LIVE....forever...with Him! Those who call upon the name of the Lord are saved! He came not to condemn the world but to save the world. He is for us...not against us...His burden is easy and His yoke is light...He has been tempted in every way and understands our struggle with sin...He is Jesus...the Savior of the world...the Prince of Peace...our every need...our Comforter...our Healer...our Friend! Happy Easter everyone!!!!

## In Christ Alone...

Nothing can steal the joy in my heart today...not even this nasty cold I have. It's EASTER!!!! I love Easter...maybe even more than Christmas. Both are special days of celebration, but Easter has a special significance...not to mention that merchandisers have yet to capitalize on this celebration of love and victory! Ok...enough of that soap box!

I have been thinking all morning long about what Easter means to me and, more specifically, what THIS Easter means to my family. As you might suspect...we are exceptionally thankful for life this year!!! The word that has come to mind most frequently today is HOPE. The motto of the Preston Robert Tisch Brain Tumor Center at Duke is...At Duke there is hope. People from all over the Unites States, and maybe the world, travel to Durham, NC looking for hope...hope that they have a chance to live...hope that they have a chance to conquer the sentence of death that looms over them...hope that someone there has the answers to their questions and medical needs.

We are so incredibly thankful for Duke, but we have never lost sight of where our hope is found...IN CHRIST ALONE! God has set eternity in our hearts...a yearning for Him and an understanding of His eternal existence (Ecc. 3). Our hearts cannot deny it, but we can certainly look to things other than Him to satisfy this yearning and realization of His existence and place of authority in our lives. Unless our hearts are tuned into Him, we are certain to be led astray on a hopeless journey. I know...I once traveled on that path! Maybe you have too and you can testify to the truth that only Christ can satisfy this deep yearning in your heart. Maybe you are currently traveling that path...are you ready to turn your eyes (and your heart) to Him. If you will just look in His face, everything else will pale in comparison to His glory and grace.

HOPE...it is something we need...something He gives!!!! Our hope is not in the cross...it is in an empty cross and an empty tomb!!!! Jesus conquered sin and death so that we might have hope...hope of eternal life...hope of conquering the bondage of sin...hope of one day spending eternity with Him...apart from sin...apart from pain...apart from suffering...hope that, even as we live in this fallen world, we can experience His love and grace and escape the temptations of this world and the snares our enemy sets for us. The tomb could not hold Him and it will not hold those who place their trust in Him!!!!

At Duke...there is hope that God will use the amazing minds of some incredible doctors to heal Mike from his cancer. BUT...in Christ, and Christ alone, there is hope that nothing can ever separate us from

God's love and an eternity of experiencing that love! In Christ ALONE our hope is found!!!!!

## Showers Of Love...

I couldn't let this monumental day pass by without a post! One year ago today, our world was rocked and life in the Hearn home changed forever. Some of the changes have been difficult; some have been the greatest blessings of our lives. Nonetheless...life changed.

Change happens! There is no escaping it. Sometimes changes are subtle and bring little to no challenge; others stir up a mountain of fear, dread, frustration, confusion, and a host of other dreadful, uncomfortable emotions. How we respond to change is key! Will we fight it and become bound by it, or will we roll with it and ride on the wings of His love and care? I've never really been one to control too many facets of my life in an effort to avoid or prevent change. Maybe that has served me well this year. Or...maybe I just realized there wasn't any point in trying to "control" or "prevent" these changes. Regardless of the "why", I am so grateful that we have somehow managed to find ourselves firmly planted on a foundation of faith. The storms and floods came, but our foundation was not shaken, destroyed, or moved. What a great and glorious God we have! He is our Rock...our Fortress...our Hope!

Words truly cannot express our gratitude for your love and support over this past year. Prayers, words, cards, meals, hugs, rides to treatment - each representing a shower of God's grace coming at just the right time to give us strength, comfort, or whatever we were in need of at that very moment. Each of you have been an instrument of God's love and grace.

We have recently come in contact with a family who is on a journey similar to ours. As we have corresponded with them, we have been keenly aware of how your support served as a buffer and protection from so much stress during this journey. You have no idea the burdens you have lifted...freeing Mike and I up to focus on his healing.

You have absorbed so much of our burden and for that we are eternally grateful. The only thing we know to do is pray that God blesses you 100 times over for how you have blessed us! Thank you...thank you...thank you. We love you all so very much!

**Showers of Love.....**

Showers of love fell from above
Touches of His amazing grace
A card, a meal, a hug, a prayer
Each expressions of His glorious face

Did you know our need?
Did you realize the power of your touch?
His love fell down
Our souls refreshed
Each time you reached out to us

In your face we saw His
Your words His voice
Through your kindness we felt His touch

Had it not been for you
Our souls might have withered
Our hearts might have struggled to believe

But we could not deny
His hand in our lives
As we danced in the showers of your love!

Abundantly grateful...

# Miracles...

Today is another day of celebration in the Hearn home! One year ago today, an angel by the name of Dr. Joshua Miller performed a craniotomy on Mike (I could have written operation, but craniotomy just sounds way more cool!). A GBM tumor a bit bigger than a golf ball was removed from his front left lobe. Surgery was a huge success and, contrary to most cases, the tumor came out almost perfectly intact and encapsulated. What a miracle!

I lead the lower school devotion time at our school each Monday morning. Today...I talked about miracles. Dictionary.com defines *miracle* as "an effect or extraordinary event in the physical world that surpasses all known human or natural powers and is ascribed to a supernatural cause." Even the kindergartners at FBA were able to tell me the true definition of a miracle...something that only God can do!...and to that I say...AMEN!

Only our great and glorious God can calm our hearts in the midst of this storm. Only our great and glorious God is worthy of the praise that is constantly in our hearts and on our tongues as we recount the days of this past year. Only our great and glorious God deserves credit for the many miracles we have witnessed on this journey.

During our devotion this morning, we talked about the purpose of miracles. I could not have said it any better than one of our students..."to show God's power"! That is so true! They are not simply to give us what we want or to make our lives easier or our circumstances more desirable. They are to show God's amazing power and evidence of His incredible love and providence in and over our lives...to display His glory and to demonstrate the lengths that He will go to in order to bless His creation. But...oh how we do benefit from His miracles...and for that I am so eternally grateful!

When I asked the students what we should do in response to observing God's miracles, we all agreed...we should TELL others...shout from the highest mountain and lowest valley for all to hear and see the goodness and greatness of God. If our hearts have been opened to the

Truth of the gospel and reality of God's amazing love in Jesus...we are a miracle. This is perhaps one of the greatest miracles of all...a heart changed and made alive by His love. If that is us then we must TELL! We must proclaim the goodness and greatness of God and tell others about the miracle of how He has changed our hearts...rescued us from darkness and eternal condemnation.

So...be a miracle today! Be evidence of His touch on your life...evidence of something that can only be accomplished by His power! I am so thankful that Mike is a miracle...

## Growing Pains...

A couple of days ago, Mallory mentioned that she was having growing pains in her legs. I remember having those as a pre-teen. My ankles and legs would just throb at night. Well...it seems as though she is also experiencing some spiritual growth pains. This is so painful to watch as a parent, but at the same time, so comforting to know that God is working in her life and growing her in her faith.

A week or so ago, Mallory received an assignment to prepare a class devotion. She decided she would do her devotion about trusting God and how this past year has given her opportunities to grow in her faith in and knowledge of Him. She has mentioned several times over the past year how a specific message given by our student pastor has strengthened and encouraged her and she decided she would use the scriptures he taught on in her devotion. She planned to relate all of this to dealing with Mike's cancer and how this circumstance has affected our family and her faith.

Well...when there is growth...there is often pain. While I was teaching algebra, there was a knock on my door. It was Mallory...in tears. While sharing her devotion, the walls came tumbling down and her deeply buried emotions were exposed. Bless her heart! More growing pains! But this time, Tylenol was not a viable remedy. But...a big hug from mom was. I just stood in the hall and held her while she cried.

*"Dear brothers and sisters, when troubles come your way, consider it an opportunity for great joy. For you know that when your faith is tested, your endurance has a chance to grow. So let it grow, for when your endurance is fully developed, you will be perfect and complete, needing nothing."* (James 1:2-4, NLT). Can my sweet little girl understand these words? Absolutely! As the Spirit of God speaks to her heart, she most certainly can! She is stronger now...she is not lacking what she needs at this moment! God is growing her and developing endurance.

Developing endurance is not fun! For that very reason...I've never become a runner! I am a wimp and cannot stand the burning in my lungs and stitch in my side. I give up...and therefore...have never developed the endurance and the lungs needed to run long distances.

From the moment we found out about Mike's condition, our prayer has been that God would surround and protect Davis and Mallory's hearts...that He would not allow this trial to drive a wedge between them and Him. He has been SOOOOO faithful in answering those earnest prayers! Thank you Jesus for loving my children and protecting their hearts! Thank you that I do not have to carry that burden...you know their every need! You know their hearts...you created their hearts and know them intimately! Thank you, thank you, thank you!!!!!

So...what can I learn from this? The result of growing pains is beneficial and worth the discomfort! So..."*In all this [we] greatly rejoice, though now for a little while [we] may have had to suffer grief in all kinds of trials. These have come so that the proven genuineness of [our] faith—of greater worth than gold, which perishes even though refined by fire—may result in praise, glory and honor when Jesus Christ is revealed.*" (I Peter 1:6-7) Oh how I pray my children will come out of this fire with a more genuine faith...a treasure that is worth so much more than any earthly treasure! The fires and trials of life cannot destroy things of eternal value...treasures that come from our heavenly Father!

Mike's platelets were still below 100 on Monday so no chemo this week. He heads back tomorrow to retest and will most likely start chemo on Monday, May 9. His birthday is Sunday, May 8. Last year on his birthday, we got the call from the neurosurgeon confirming his suspicions about what the pathology report would show. We anticipate that this year's birthday will be much less "eventful". I'd settle for downright boring!!!!

Running with endurance (or trying to at least)...

## *Noise...*

This world is such a noisy place! It is difficult to escape the chaos and commotion. Sometimes the noise is in my mind – stress...responsibilities...worries. It is often impossible to escape to a quiet place, whether physically or mentally. I wonder what it must have been like in the garden of Eden before the fall. Was there a constant, refreshing breeze; soft, cool grass; the fragrance of flowers; the sound of water? I imagine it as such a quiet, peaceful place where the noise is not chaotic but serene and relaxing. That is until Satan came into the picture and filled the hearts and minds of Adam and Eve with the noise of doubt and disobedience and their lives with the consequences and shame of their sins.

This past year has been a "noisy" one! I'm a person who craves quiet...moments to calm my mind and listen to God's voice of comfort, peace, wisdom, love, and strength. In fact, this has been an exceptionally "noisy" week. It's chemo week, school is winding down and the natives are restless...I need a "Calgon" moment!

The thing I hate the most about the noise of this world is that it makes it much more difficult to hear God's voice. We must work to create moments of solitude and serenity in order to walk in the garden with God. Tonight, I needed one of those moments. When we got home from church, I grabbed my tennis shoes and iPod, determined to escape the noise. This is definitely one of my favorite ways to escape...into songs of praise...songs that speak to my soul...songs that magnify the cry of my heart and speak Truth into my life.

God calls us to be still and KNOW. If only it were that easy! Sure...just drop everything and be still. Drop the chemo...drop the job...drop the laundry...drop the grading papers...drop the making tests and lesson plans...drop everything and just be still.  The reality is...we can be still in our *hearts*...we can quiet our minds and press into the heart of God and hear His still small voice even in the midst of the chaos of life. I find it interesting that God has such a still small voice when He speaks to my heart, but at the same time, almost instantly, His soft tender voice can shatter the chaos and overpower the things that drown Him out and distract my attention and trust. Still and small, but so commanding and powerful is the voice of our Savior! I guess that is because He is never frantic or controlled by emotions...He's calm, sure, sovereign, and tender! The whisper of His voice calms my anxious heart like nothing else!

For me...one of the sure fire ways to escape the noise and chaos of this world is to sing His praises. This just lifts my soul above the chaos...above the noise! It allows me to BE STILL and KNOW and to hear His voice above all else...even in the midst of this noisy world!  God reminded me of all this through a song tonight - *Keep Singing* by Mercy Me[17]. Here are the lyrics to this beautiful song. I hope it will encourage you to KEEP SINGING and find moments to be still and KNOW in this crazy, chaotic, noisy world we live in and especially in the moments when chaos and noise creeps into your heart and mind.  It is so important to find moments to escape into His love and let Him sing over us with songs of peace.

**Keep Singing...**

Another rainy day
I can't recall having sunshine on my face
All I feel is pain
All I wanna do is walk out of this place
But when I am stuck and I can't move
When I don't know what I should do
When I wonder if I'll ever make it through

I gotta keep singing
I gotta keep praising Your name
You're the one that's keeping my heart beating
I gotta keep singing
I gotta keep praising Your name
That's the only way that I'll find healing

Can I climb up in Your lap
I don't wanna leave
Jesus sing over me
I gotta keep singing

Can I climb up in Your lap
I don't wanna leave
Jesus sing over me
I gotta keep singing

Oh You're everything I need
And I gotta keep singing

Mike is doing well this week. Things usually start to get rough for him around Wednesday night or Thursday during chemo week. He's feeling a big queasy, but other than that, doing well. He just seems to buckle his seat belt and endure the ride. He's a trooper...up every morning to help with the kids and see them off to school...picks them up from school as long as he's not too loopy to drive...helps with dinner and keeping the kids organized with homework. I am amazed by his strength and resolve! We appreciate your prayers and encouragement as well as the many birthday wishes!

Resting in a quiet place...

## *Living In The Here And Now...*

     This morning was a weepy time for me...for many reasons! Let me just go ahead and warn you...this might be a lengthy post! God has placed a lot on my heart today. For those of you who choose to endure my rambling, I hope and pray He blesses you half as much as He has blessed me today with His tender voice and soothing love.

     One of the things that got me going this morning was seeing a group of young children singing in front of our congregation during worship. As I sat there and looked at the sweet, adorable faces of the boys and girls, I was taken back to memories of Davis and Mallory at that age. Davis' sweet little face and big heart...Mallory's innocent smile and big bow in her hair just like the little girls who stood before me. It was just more than I could handle. Oh how I miss those days. Where has time gone? Did I waste precious moments with my children? Did I really cherish and embrace those days of being a mother of pre-schoolers? I would have given anything this morning to go back in time!

     Unfortunately, we cannot go back in time. Besides, we have wonderful times in the here and now to enjoy. Each stage is special in its own way (yes...even adolescence!). Thankfully, we have memories tucked in the recesses of our mind and we can travel back in time, so to speak, whenever we choose. God reminded me this morning to not only enjoy the here and now, but to take time to cherish memories...to not let the "sweetness" of those years end up in a dusty corner of my mind.

I don't know what the future holds, or just how many opportunities we will have to make memories as a family. The truth is..none of us do. So why do we spend so much time longing for and worrying about the future only to one day long to go back in time and cherish the days we spent focused on what is to come?

Then, I began to wonder...are these just my thoughts? Is the Lord really taking me to this sappy, weepy place to teach me something, or am I just having "one of those days" when reality is slapping me in the face. So...I searched the scripture to see if my thoughts could be found in God's Word...and here is what I found...

*"Look here, you who say, "Today or tomorrow we are going to a certain town and will stay there a year. We will do business there and make a profit." How do you know what your life will be like tomorrow? Your life is like the morning fog—it's here a little while, then it's gone. What you ought to say is, "If the Lord wants us to, we will live and do this or that." Otherwise you are boasting about your own plans, and all such boasting is evil. Remember, it is sin to know what you ought to do and then not do it." James 4:13-17 NLT*

Challenging words...and we know that God's word is living and active...sharper than a two edged sword...and these words cut to the heart today! It is a sin to know what the Lord is calling us to do and to ignore it. We are called to live in the here and now and aware of what God is calling us to do each and every day...not consumed with what our future will be like or how our life will be better in the future and more fitting to God's plan. Enjoy life now! Seek the Lord while He can be found! Lean not on our own understanding, but allow Him to direct our paths. Don't worry about tomorrow! Trust that He sees the big picture and will provide our every need when it comes about.

WOW! I can honestly say, I have not lived my life fully devoted to His plans. I've been selfish...I've been fearful...I've been lazy...I've been discontent! Nothing like a healthy dose of reality to help me see all this. Thank you, Lord! I thank you that cancer has helped me to live more in the here and now...cherishing every moment...even when my kids are being true to their little adolescent selves...ha!

193

We are not promised tomorrow. It'll be great if it comes, but why not cherish what we have today...that way...we have no regrets...but we have a treasure trove of beautiful memories and a heart that is blessed by knowing we have made our Father smile!

I've been overwhelmed by God's goodness today...to the point of tears...tears of joy...tears of gratitude...tears of faith and trust and indescribable peace. Overwhelmed by His tender, on time love and grace. Lord...I'm amazed by You!

Mike survived another round of chemo! ONLY 3 MORE ROUNDS!!!!! WOW! He is so excited! We are all getting excited about heading to Indiana. It will be a wonderful time to relax and have some overdue family time. No schedules...no early bedtimes...no homework...just time to hang out and make some special memories to tuck away in our hearts. Indiana has a special place in both our hearts. It is not only "home" for Mike, but it is also where we started our married life together, where we both were saved and discipled as baby Christians, and a place we've come to find as a refuge and retreat where God never fails to meet with us in a special way. There's just something about the beauty of the surroundings and tranquility that cultivate times of deep fellowship with Christ. We are counting the days!

## *Things Unseen...*

Living in this broken, fallen world makes it difficult sometimes to believe the word of God! Not that it isn't completely true and trustworthy, but difficult for us weak and fickle humans to *choose* to *believe* it and *trust* it completely. Even the disciples doubted Jesus. Last Sunday's message at my church was centered on John 20 – the well-known account of Thomas struggling to believe that Jesus had indeed been resurrected. I've always felt kind of sorry for Thomas. I am not so sure that I would not have struggled to believe if I were in his place. It wasn't that he did not WANT to believe...he was just having a difficult time finding the *faith* to believe...without proof...without seeing.

194

As we have traveled down this unfamiliar path, there have been many moments when we have struggled to believe and "demanded" proof for our eyes when our hearts did not have the strength to fight the fears and doubts of what our future might look like. When left with only what our earthly eyes can see...faith is sometimes hard to muster! But...is it really faith if God has to prove to our eyes what our heart should believe?

Hebrews 11 is one of my favorite passages of scripture...the heroes of faith. Hebrews 11:1-3 says that *"Faith is the confidence that what we hope for will actually happen; it gives us assurance about things we cannot see. Through their faith, the people in days of old earned a good reputation. By faith we understand that the entire universe was formed at God's command, that what we now see did not come from anything that can be seen." (NLT).* This chapter of Hebrews goes on to recount amazing examples of faith in scripture. It highlights the determined and faithful actions of individuals just like you and me. I've always been inspired by their actions; however, the verse that always stands out to me most in Hebrews 11 is verse 39... *"All these people earned a good reputation because of their faith, yet none of them received all that God had promised."* They kept on believing even though what they knew to be true did not necessarily match up with what their eyes could see. Now that is the true definition of faith...believing without seeing.

Remember Thomas...did he get a bad rap? I think so. After all...who among us has not had a moment of doubt when life was kicking us in the tail? At least Thomas was willing to believe...he was just at a moment when he needed proof for his eyes...maybe the eyes of his heart were just too full of tears as he grieved the loss of his Friend, Teacher, and Savior. I know I've been there many times this past year. Moments when I just had to cry out to the Lord and say, "Lord, I am struggling to believe. Could you just prove to my eyes what my heart is struggling to believe?" He always comes through! Just as He did for Thomas. His plan is not to hang us out to dry. Does He tarry sometimes? Yes! Remember, it took Him 4 days to arrive at the grave of

195

Lazarus...a time when Mary and Martha were struggling to believe. However, when He tarries, there is good reason! I personally believe His choice to tarry is so that we can believe even more deeply.

It is my prayer that the Lord will open up my eyes to things unseen...to sharpen the vision of the eyes of my heart. I want to have unwavering faith even when my circumstances do not seem to match up to what I know in my heart to be true. The truth is...sometimes my heart is willing but my flesh is weak. Maybe I've just relied too much on my eyes to see more often than I've looked at life through the eyes of my heart.

I don't know what the future holds today any more than I did one year ago. Yes...Mike is doing well and yes he has had clean MRI's and a clean PET scan, but that cannot be where my faith and hope are found. My hope must be built on nothing less that Jesus' blood and righteousness. What is seen is temporary, but what is unseen is eternal (II Corinthians 4:18). How foolish I would be to place my faith in something that is temporary!

So...today...let's all ask the Lord to open up our eyes to the things unseen...to give us a glimpse of the eternal...of His glory...of His face. If we do...I know our hearts will be filled with His peace that passes all understanding...with a passion to live for Him...with a sense of awe of who He is...a sense of wonder as we are immersed in and captivated by His love. Let's turn our eyes to Jesus...look straight into His loving face...and everything else in this world will soon pale in comparison to His beautiful glory and grace!

# *Your Story...*

Even when we relentlessly trust God and resolve to rest in His love and grace, going through a trial can be painful and exhausting. Can you relate? Maybe you feel like you are hanging on by a thread and barely trudging along on this journey of faith. That is OK! God knows your heart! He knows your every need! If you seek Him with **all** your heart and **determine** to follow Him, He will give you peace, and that peace will continue to guard your heart! Take some time to record some thoughts related to how you have experienced God's amazing peace in the midst of your storms. Or...maybe you need to cry out to the Lord and ask Him to help you understand what it means to rest in His peace...to trust Him completely during the trials of life. He's waiting...

Chapter Twelve

# *Resting...*

*"Yes, my soul, find rest in God; my hope comes from him."*
*Psalm 62:5*

In a few days, summer vacation will begin. I cannot wait. Although this has been an exciting year full of miracles and blessings...I am worn out! I am ready to rest a while. I am looking forward to sleeping in, reading, drowning out the "noise" of this world with my iPod, soaking up the sun, strolling through the Amish flea market, picking blueberries...it's gonna be great!

One of my summer traditions is reading the book *Hinds' Feet On High Places*[18]. For some reason, this sweet little story about the character Much Afraid and her Great Shepherd speaks to my heart. If you have not read it, I highly recommend it! It is an allegory that beautifully illustrates the longing of every believer's heart to escape the struggles and perils of this world to the peaceful high places where we are free to live in fellowship with our King and high above all that hinders us. Here is a little excerpt from the book that always grabs my attention and heart...

*"As Christians, we know, in theory at least, that in the life of a child of God there are no second causes, that even the most unjust and cruel things, as well as all the seemingly pointless and undeserved sufferings, have been permitted by God as a glorious opportunity for us to react to them in such a way that our Lord and Savior is able to produce in us, little by little, His own lovely character...the High Places of victory and union with Christ cannot be reached by any mental reckoning of self to be dead to sin, or by seeking to devise some way or discipline by which we can be crucified. The only way is by learning to accept, day by day, the actual conditions and tests permitted by God, by a continually repeated laying down of our own will and acceptance of His as it is presented to us in the form of the people with whom we have to live and work, and in the things which happen to us. Every acceptance of His will becomes an altar of sacrifice, and every such surrender and abandonment of ourselves to His will as a means of furthering us on the way to the High Places to which He desires to bring every child of His while they are still living on earth."*

Wow! Do those words not just grab your heart and cause you to long for and yearn for such a place...a high place to escape to even while still living in the midst of this fallen, broken world? That should be our pursuit...*to trust our Savior so completely that we are willing to accept any sort of suffering and still manage to rise above it all and dwell on the high places of complete trust and security and gratefulness.* Imagine how victoriously we would live if we resolved each day to have this level of surrender and sacrifice. How absolutely freeing it would be to refuse to allow the burdens and troubles of this world to drag us down into a pit of self-pity, doubt, fear, or dread. If only it were **easy** to allow adversity to fuel our faith and strengthen us in a way that would allow us to bound effortlessly to the mountain top. Lord...give me the feet of a swift gazelle...hinds' feet...so that I may rest with you in high places!

Mike has completed 9 rounds of treatment in his clinical trial. There were times I wondered if he would ever make it to such a milestone...physically and emotionally! Nonetheless, here we are with the finish line in sight, trying our best to find that final burst of energy to carry us through...that final push...that sprint to the finish line. We are almost there and we can feel the adrenaline starting to build up in our veins.

Yes...we will finish strong...

## When Things Don't Make Sense...

Life is so easy to understand and accept when our circumstances fall within the realm of our own human wisdom and reasoning. But...what about when life just doesn't make sense? Will we stay stuck in the vortex of searching for answers we may never find or will we rest in what we KNOW to be true?

Throughout this journey, we have prayed and seen God do amazing things – things that defy any explanation other than God's mighty and miraculous hand. We have felt His touch and heard His voice like never before. At times we have walked blindly on this

201

unfamiliar path only certain that our very next step was secure and trusting that God was leading us into safety rather than off a steep cliff. Other times, He has lit our path up like a runway...clearly illuminating not only our next step, but also the path that lie ahead of us.

Then, there were the times that we had absolutely no idea what God was doing or WHY He was allowing certain things to take place. It was in those moments that we had to turn from our desire to *understand why* and just trust what we *know to be true*. I believe this is a common struggle for us all...learning to trust God's wisdom and accepting that His ways are much higher than ours and that His wisdom far exceeds ours. There are just going to be those times that we must accept the "I don't know why" moments of life and trust the truth's that we have tucked into our hearts. Truths like Romans 8:28...Psalm 37:4...Proverbs 3:5&6...and the list goes on.

We recently became acquainted with a couple in Indiana who are on a journey similar to ours. The husband was diagnosed with a GBM last fall, had surgery, and was receiving the standard treatment protocol. Around six months into his treatment, the cancer returned. He had another surgery to remove the recurring tumor and was told by the doctors in his home town that they had done pretty much all they could do for him. This past week, he traveled to Duke and received encouraging news and returned home with a new sense of **hope**. This past Sunday, he began having some symptoms that concerned him and his wife. They drove to a hospital in a larger town nearby and he collapsed when they got to the ER. He was bleeding in his brain and had to have surgery. The doctors said had he not come to the ER he would have probably died. He was taken off the ventilator today and is speaking and making sense.

This is one of those circumstances when I would love to scream, "Why, Lord? Why in the world would you allow this to happen after such a positive, encouraging trip to Duke?" In fact, I am sure in my heart, I did. Immediately, the Lord reminded me of what a slippery slope it is to question His will and to try and make sense of things through my finite wisdom. Instead, I needed to immediately turn to praising Him and claiming what I know to be true...His ways are perfect...He is sovereign over all...He is faithful...He is for this family and not against them...if He allows this, He has a purpose in it!

James 1 reminds us to face our trials with joy...knowing that God is perfecting our faith, refining us of any spiritual impurities. We are also reminded to ask God for wisdom. We should ask God, trust that He will give it to us, and then stand on our faith and believe, not doubt. Does believing mean that we know every detail and have all our "why's" answered? I don't think so. I believe that, in these verses, God is reminding us to believe HIM and all that we know to be true about HIM. When we do so, the storms of life and waves of doubt will not toss us about in confusion. Instead, we will be firmly anchored and able to ride out the storm to safety! It is in the promises of God that we can find peaceful rest for our souls!

### When Things Don't Make Sense

When things don't make sense
Lord, protect my heart
Cast out all my fears and doubts

Life can be cruel
Your wisdom I lack
Yet my heart demands to know why

Will I trust you with all
Will I rest in your love
Will I stand firm on the promises you've made

When things don't make sense
Lord, protect my heart
Help me know that my life is in your hands

Mike has had a wonderful week. He is feeling great! It has been a busy week, but a great week so far. Today was the kids last day of school. We are all looking forward to summer and spending some quality time together. Last summer, Mike was going to radiation treatments 5 days a week and taking chemo. We are looking forward to a much more enjoyable summer vacation this year!!!! To top it off...as summer passes us by and winds down...Mike will also be winding down his clinical trial at Duke and this phase of his treatments will come to an end! Praise the Lord. For once...we will be excited for summer to be over because that means Dad is done with chemo!!!!!!

Ready for some rest...

## Freedom In Helplessness...

I was reminded this past week of some thoughts that the Lord gave me almost a year ago...the reality that there is such freedom in our helplessness. One of the greatest lies of the enemy is that we can somehow manage this life and all our troubles on our own. When we take the bait and believe this lie, we are trapped in the snare of self-reliance...a facade...a fragile state of delusion that will eventually come crashing down, leaving us in a state of fear, frustration, and confusion the moment we face troubles that require great faith in God and a complete surrender to His will. But...praise the Lord, when we have placed our faith and trust in Jesus, we are forever in His mighty grip and tender care.

In my current circumstances, I am completely helpless! However, I am no more helpless today than I was 1 year ago...2 years ago...5 years ago. The only difference is that a year or so ago, I *thought* I was much more in control of things than I truly was! My *perception* was flawed, my view of *reality* was distorted. The truth is, we are all helpless and in need of the One who helps us.

There is such freedom in recognizing and accepting helplessness! Our enemy taunts us and tempts us to buy into the lie that we are capable of managing our lives and providing for ourselves. The TRUTH is...it was never intended to be that way. God's original and perfect plan was for us to be completely dependent upon Him. His desire was for us to walk with Him and come to Him for our every need and desire to be fulfilled. From the beginning of time, Satan knew this and it infuriated him (still does!). He is completely and utterly jealous of our relationship with God and His crazy love for us. Just as Satan tempted Adam and Eve to "determine" for themselves what was best and most satisfying, he does the same with us. He lures us into thinking that we know what is best, that we can solve our problems, that we can secure a job, that we can provide for our families, that we have the intellect and skills to figure things out on our own. When all along, God asks us to cast all our cares upon Him and to allow Him to bear the burden and provide the solutions to all our needs. We feel the burdens of life, but we were never intended to carry them and solve them alone. Like a little child who completely trusts and looks to his parents to care for him and solve all his problems, we should also look first to our heavenly Father to do the same. And He will!

There is FREEDOM in helplessness! Freedom from fear, freedom from worry, freedom from pride, freedom from compromise, freedom from anything that would entangle us and cause us to miss the abundant, beautiful, and completely satisfying life God has in store for us! This realization has been one that God has used time and time again over the past year to strengthen and encourage our hearts. At times we have struggled to surrender to this realization, but, for the most part, we have rested in the peace it brings!

He is faithful and He will not fail us! What a great and glorious God we have! How He loves us so!

Resting in my helplessness...

# *His Ways...*

His ways are definitely higher than our ways...thank goodness for that! Otherwise, we would worship a God who is easily understood by our human minds and we would most likely find a way to ultimately be our own gods. Throughout time, men have attempted to reduce God down to something they could understand and "control". In Romans 1 we read about those who traded truth for lies and worshiped and served the created verses the Creator. In an attempt to become wise...they became foolish! I am sure I have fallen into that trap a time or two! In an attempt to "make sense of things", I am certain that I have sought comfort and confidence from my own wisdom and intellect, all the while falling into a trap of foolishness and a false sense of peace.

Throughout this journey, Mike and I have been blessed to meet some fellow sojourners who are traveling paths similar to ours...paths that are passing through the great unknown of cancer...more specifically...brain cancer. At the moment, we are watching several of them struggle and fight for their lives. We are also watching some come to the end of their journey and fight with this nasty disease. "Why's" swirl through our minds as we seek to understand God's will and purpose in allowing them to suffer or lose their battle with brain cancer. These are amazing men and women of God who have faith to move mountains and have cried out to the Lord for physical healing. So...why, Lord? Why has their journey taken them into the valley of the shadow of death? What is your purpose in their suffering? And dare I ask...why them and not us? We are eternally grateful for how God has answered our prayers, but there is a part of me that wonders why...a part of me that would like to understand why God answers some prayers according to our desires and some in ways we cannot understand or comprehend...ways that seem the polar opposite of what we ask for.

To be honest, it is difficult to watch these new friends suffer and face the end of their journey. It is a glaring reminder of the reality of Mike's fight - a constant reminder of the statistics that we have been so certain God can and will overcome in order to accomplish His will in this

206

mess. At the same time, it has been a reminder to give God all the glory and honor and praise for the progress Mike is making and for his miraculous good health.

Our hearts ache for those we know who are facing the reality of how difficult it is to beat a GBM brain tumor. BUT...in the end...we all win! When we have placed our hope and faith in Jesus Christ, WE WIN! This world is not our home...we are just passing through. That must be our perspective if we hope to faithfully worship and serve the Creator rather than the created! He is our hope...He is our peace...He is our prize!

Brad, Lisa, and Jennifer...we love you and we are praying for you and your families! Keep fighting...keep believing...keep loving and trusting Jesus! He has a plan and purpose for every detail of your life! He has a purpose for your pain! Nothing will ever separate you from His love!

## Cancer Won't Win!

I love teaching science. It provides so many opportunities for me to point to the awesome power of God and evidence of His divine creation. It is exciting to see my students discover the many ways creation supports the Truth found in the Bible. In some instances, I've seen students struggle to reconcile contradictions between their pre-established worldly wisdom and beliefs with evidence we uncover as we study our world and science from a biblical perspective...science sifted through Truth rather than Truth sifted through science.

I recall teaching about our solar system last year and trying to illustrate to my students how the earth revolves around the sun and how the earth spins on its axis thus causing changes in our seasons and how day changes into night and night into day. A few students struggled to grasp the concepts I was teaching. Why? Well...because what I was teaching was contrary to what they "saw". Each day, they "saw" the sun rise and set and move around the earth. On the other hand, they could not "see" the earth spinning on its axis. Therefore, the earth must be fixed and the sun revolving around it...right?  We all know the answer to that...absolutely NOT!

When it comes to matters of life and faith, our hearts are often deceived by what we "see". We have a difficult time reconciling the contradiction between our "reality" and what the Word says is true.  We must believe with our hearts and not our eyes! Sometimes, life gets in the way and distorts our view.  Think about when you look into the sky at the sun...it looks so small...but it is hardly small...it is ginormous compared to our tiny little planet.  If you stick your thumb up in from of your face, it will probably appear as though your thumb is covering up the sun...now that is what I call a distorted perception/view...but it does nothing to change the TRUTH...the sun is still ginormous!

As we have traveled this unfamiliar path, there have been many instances when things have stood between us and God, blocking our view of Him and, to be honest, making Him look small.  Thankfully, we have been able to quickly change our position of faith and remove the obstacles that stood between us and God...obstacles that distorted our view of His bigness...His faithfulness...His love...His grace.

Cancer is a nasty disease!  Mike is fighting for his life, but our BIG GOD is also fighting for Him.  I wonder if when Goliath stood before David that his view of God became distorted...if just for a moment...was David's view of God blocked by the bigness of this giant?  Well...even if it was, in the end, David managed to use his stones of truth to defeat his enemy and remove what stood between God and him...and that is what we have to do when our giants stand between us and God, distorting our view. We must be transformed by the renewing of our minds (Romans 12:1-2), thus removing anything that stands between us and our Lord.

I spent a couple of hours today at the hospital with Emily Hemmer.  Emily's husband, Brad, is fighting GBM cancer, too. He is in a rough place right now, and it would be easy for Emily's perspective of God to be distorted by some mighty big obstacles.  Instead, I saw a woman who has refused to let her circumstances come between her and her God!  Are her circumstances full of giant obstacles...YES!  However,

Emily has managed to refuse to allow these obstacles to come between her and her Lord!  She clearly sees the bigness of God! Brain cancer is a ruthless, nasty enemy, but it cannot beat the soul that has placed its hope in God!  Cancer has stolen a great deal from the Hemmer family, but the eternal things...the things that matter most...remain!

**Cancer Won't Win...**

Fighting for your life
Your enemy strong and cruel

It knocks you down again and again
Your life it longs to rule

At times you grow weary
Longing to give in

Just in time
Faith rises up
Cancer won't win

It longs to isolate you
Whispering words of doubt

If only it could distract you
Convince you there's no hope

But on the other side
Beyond the giant you fight
Stands your mighty King
Full of power and might

Cancer can't conceal His love
Cancer's not that big

So sling your stones
Your enemy will fall
Your hope remains in Him

Open the eyes of your heart
Remember what you know to be true

With only a seed of faith...trusting in His grace
***Cancer WILL NOT win!!!!!!!!***

## *Tis So Sweet...*

Tis so sweet to trust in Jesus
Just to take Him at His word
Just to rest upon His promise
And to know "Thus saith the Lord!"[19]

The word rest has so many meanings. It not only refers to the physical but also the spiritual. Our bodies can be in a complete state of rest, but our hearts and minds can continue striving and worrying. On the other hand, we can be in a state of physical busyness as we navigate our circumstances yet our hearts and minds can remain at rest when we abide in and trust Jesus. I'll take the latter any day over the former!

The number one goal for our family this summer is to rest...to rest physically, but most important spiritually. Over the past year, the "busyness" of life has served as a wonderful distraction from the chaos that has entered into our lives as a result of Mike's cancer. As our physical lives settle down this summer, it would be easy for our hearts and minds to be tossed to and fro by our circumstances without the distractions of busyness. Instead, our goal is total and complete rest.

There is nothing sweeter than the feeling of being so tucked into God's love that our hearts and minds experience His perfect peace. That is the greatest state of rest there is...regardless of our physical circumstances to be able to find peace and serenity as we rest in Him...our shelter and refuge in times of trouble.

*"Rest in God alone, my soul, for my hope comes from Him. He alone is my rock and my salvation, my stronghold; I will not be shaken. My salvation and glory depend on God; my strong rock, my refuge, is in God. Trust in Him at all times, you people; pour out your hearts before Him. God is our refuge. Selah."* Psalm 62:5-8 HCSB

I have a little sign in our home that reads...Great strength comes from great faith in God. So true! I think I need another sign to say...It takes great strength to have faith in God! Sometimes that is the case...it takes great strength to have the kind of faith that brings peace to our souls. Then again...that type of great strength can only COME **from** God and believing Him...taking Him at His word.

Regardless of what life brings our way, we can all find rest for our hearts and minds...but not from the things of this world like medicine, job security, a spouse, a strong bank account or 401K. The rest our souls long for can only come from resting in Him...taking Him at His word...trusting in His promises. Even in the midst of great pain or uncertainty, we can find rest!

### Jesus I am Resting, Resting

Jesus I am resting, resting
In the Joy of what Thou art;
I am finding out the greatness
Of Thy loving heart.

Thou hast bid me gaze upon Thee,
And Thy beauty fills my soul,
For by Thy transforming power
Thou hast made me whole.

Jesus, I am resting, resting

211

In the joy of what Thou art;
I am finding out the greatness
Of Thy loving heart.

O how great Thy loving kindness.
Vaster, broader than the sea!
O how marvelous Thy goodness,
Lavished all on me!

Yes, I rest in Thee, Beloved,
Know Thy certainty of promise,
And have made it mine.

Simply trusting Thee, Lord Jesus,
I behold Thee as Thou art,
And Thy love, so pure, so changeless,
Satisfies my heart;

Satisfies its deepest longings,
Meets supplies its every need,
Compasseth me round with blessings;
Thine is love indeed!

Ever lift Thy face upon me,
As I work and wait for Thee;
Resting 'neath Thy smile, Lord Jesus,
Earth's dark shadows flee.

Brightness of my Father's glory,
Sunshine of my Father's face,
Keep me ever trusting, resting;
Fill me with Thy grace.[20]

I just love that song. The words are so true and such a beautiful reminder of the true meaning of rest...trusting in Jesus and being filled with the grace He so lavishly gives each and every day! Easy...NO! Worth it...YES! He is faithful and He will do His part...if only we will let go and trust...we WILL rest!

# A New Place Of Freedom...

Freedom has been an aspect of salvation that I have grown to love throughout my walk with Christ. Before I knew Him, and for some time after coming to know Him, I lived in bondage to so many things...my past, my choices, lies about who I was and where my worth was found. Over the years, I have found freedom that can only come from abiding in Christ and refusing to allow the enemy to control my heart and mind. I am experiencing a whole new type of freedom these days brought about by the changes that have taken place in my life over the past year. I am not sure if I can even describe it. Maybe it is not even a new place; maybe I am just experiencing a more pure, genuine freedom. But...freedom from what...fear maybe, control maybe, doubt, regrets, false expectations...I'm not really sure, but something...many things...have changed. Most likely it is my perspective - a clearer, less distorted view of God and His love for me (and all of His children). Maybe I am experiencing more of the peace that comes with freedom. Yes...I think that is it...more peace!

When Mike called me that dreaded night, I thought I was going to throw up...literally. The words still echo in my head, "A lesion showed up on the MRI." "What the heck is a lesion...do you mean tumor. What does that mean exactly", was my verbal response, but I knew in my gut exactly what that meant...we were in for a ride! The first passage of scripture the Holy Spirit illuminated in my heart (thankfully His Word dwells there!) was Luke 7:18-23...with a neon sign pointing to verse 23 - "Blessed is anyone who does not stumble on account of me." Great, I thought, what exactly do you mean by that, Lord? Are You not coming through for us on this one (as we would like)? Are You encouraging us

213

to believe all that we KNOW to be true about You even though we have found ourselves in this dark and scary place? To be quite honest, I am still not sure! However, I do know this...He will NEVER leave us or forsake us! His love for us is perfect and pure and beyond our comprehension! His perfect love cast out ALL our fears as we draw close to Him and hide within the shelter of His wings. He is GOOD, and "though He slay [us]" (Job 13:15), our hope is in Him and He is sovereign over all of this! HE is mighty to save, the lifter of our heads, our shield, our comforter, our Lord, our King, our hope, our joy, our SALVATION...what more could we ask for!

So...here we are...still walking this unknown, unforeseen path. We are finding joy "in" this circumstance, and we are thankful "for" this circumstance (even though it is incredibly scary and extremely hard) because we have gained a much clearer view of God. His glory is now brighter...His love is now sweeter...His power is more magnificent...His mercy is newer...His grace is all-sufficient...His touch is more tender...His voice is clearer. I would not trade these treasures for anything...even to go back to the way life was before the "C" word.  Pressing FORWARD...I want to take hold of Jesus and all that He has taken hold of for me!

Without FREEDOM...none of this could have been accomplished in my life. Thank you, Jesus! I give YOU all the credit...all the glory...all the praise!

**Free...**

Shackled, captive, bound to lies
Born as a slave to sin
All along my heart longed for more
Determined to truly live

A seed of hope
A glimmer of love
Was all that I needed to believe

There is more to this life
I was not meant for this
If only I could escape

There must be a way
There must be a key
That will unlock the chains on my heart
The cross...yes the cross!
That is my key!
It's the answer I'm looking for!

At Calvary His cry shattered the curse
A spectacle my enemy became

It is for freedom He died
That I might live
Free from the sin and shame!

Free from fear
Free from doubt
Free from the weight of this world

Truth sets me free
Truth breaks the chains
Truth guards my wandering heart!

I cherish the freedom I have because of what Jesus did on the cross. Even though this life can be hard at times and we will continue to fail our Lord, we are still free...free to be called children of God...free to receive all that He longs to lavish on us...free from fear...free from shame...free from anything that might hinder us from experiencing all that He has planned for our lives. Let us not be taken captive again by the yoke of slavery...let us walk boldly in the freedom Christ accomplished on the cross! When we call upon the name of the Lord and invite Him to be the center of our lives...we are free...where the Spirit of the Lord is...there IS freedom! Proclaim your freedom today! Celebrate it! Throw it up in the enemy's face! If you have a relationship with Christ...freedom is yours and that cannot be taken away unless you allow the shackles to be placed back on!  No matter what life brings...freedom is ours because of the cross!

I must admit there have been times the enemy has tried to convince me that I was not really free.  He taunted me and reminded me of what it was like when I lived in bondage.  He worked hard to convince me that because I still struggled with certain issues that I was still in bondage to Him.  What a lie! We may struggle along the way, but we are not in bondage unless we allow our challenges and sins to control our lives! When the Israelites first entered the promised land, one of the first things they encountered was their enemy.  The same is true for us when we enter into a relationship with Christ. We are sure to encounter our enemy as we walk with Him, but we ARE free! God knows our weaknesses and our freedom does not depend on our pitiful strength...it depends on His amazing grace.

Praying that you live in the freedom that Jesus accomplished on the cross. He loves you and He longs for you to be FREE!

# A Dark Cloud...

A dark cloud has settled over my heart today. Sorry...this won't be one of those happy, sappy posts! Just an open, transparent spilling of my heart. I must say that this journey has not been filled with too many "dark cloud" days, and when they do roll in they are usually blown away rather quickly by God's love and grace...then the Son shines again in my heart.

I've been struggling with the loss of Lisa and Brad. I've had to fight hard not to fall into a pit of despair as I've thought about what Mark and Emily are going through right now...a pit of excessive emotional empathy for the two of them and "what if's" for me.  I have had to work hard to take my thoughts captive in order to not be swept away by a storm of fear and dread. Thankfully...God promises to rescue our hearts and minds when we call upon His name...the name of the Lord **IS** a strong tower...a refuge...a safe place to ride out the storm (Proverbs 18:10).

As I was working out this morning, I was listening to Matt Maher on my iPod. God spoke to me through his song *You Were On the Cross*[21]. A reminder that Jesus feels every bit of my pain and suffered the cross so that I might live...so that I might have victory...so that I might rise above the pain of this world through God's resurrection power. I thought about Emily when I heard these words...

"Lost, everything is lost
And everything I've loved before is gone
Alone like the coming of the frost
And a cold winter's chill in my stony heart

And where were You when all that I've hoped for?
Where You when all that I've dreamed?
Came crashing down in shambles around me
You were on the cross"

Regardless of what is causing our pain...loss, shame, loneliness, sickness, a broken heart...Jesus was on the cross so He could one day end our pain and suffering...so He could make a way for us to feel the Father's tender, comforting touch as we suffer in this world...so the Comforter could come and live in us. He was on the cross!

I've said it before...I don't like pain! But...if we can't feel pain, then likewise, we cannot feel the tender touch of God...we can't experience His healing...we can't experience the feeling of His grace washing over our lives bringing the indescribable peace that comes from knowing that He is with us and for us.

Thank you Matt Maher for touching my heart with this powerful song today. Thank You Jesus for reminding me that You felt every pain I would ever feel when You willingly placed Your life on the cross for me. Thank You God for blowing the dark clouds away with the sound of Your faithful voice in my heart!

Beating cancer (or any other trial in life) means so much more than living to see this trial completely gone from our lives. Beating cancer is much more than being healed physically. The true victory over cancer is being able to trust God completely and to find total peace in His perfect will and purpose for allowing cancer into our lives. Achieving this victory is often a bloody battle! But, thankfully, we are not the only ones fighting...Jesus, our King, is fighting for us and with us!

The Son is shining again!

## Floatin' Along...

Mike and I had the opportunity to speak at his mom and dad's church last Sunday and share a little bit about our journey this past year along this unfamiliar path. It was such a blessing and honor to speak about all that God has done for us and in us these past months; however, the greatest blessing was spending time reflecting on and recounting all the many and mighty things we have seen the Lord do. I wish I could find the words to accurately describe what I feel in my heart right now. I guess it is kind of like the scene I am looking at right now...the sun is shining down on the lake...there is not a ripple in the water...it is perfectly calm...birds are singing...flowers are blooming...a gentle breeze is blowing...all is well.

As Mike shared his side of the story, he pointed out how this past year has reminded him of how God is involved in the tiniest of details in our lives. He challenged the congregation to tune into God's still, small voice and respond to His call even when His requests "don't make sense." God has met our every need this past year, and I am sure there have been moments when He spoke to many of you and you thought, *"OK, Lord, if you say so."* It would be impossible to list the number of times one of you met a specific need for our family, never knowing that we had the need. From the big, urgent needs to the smallest and most unsuspecting need...you have touched our lives in so many ways. Potato soup will always bring a smile to our faces as we think about the multitude of times our phone rang and Mary Ruth was on the other end ready to deliver Mike some "comfort" food. It was certainly comfort for his stomach, but even more so, it was comfort for his soul as he was reminded of God's tender and on time care.

I shared about the sense of freedom I have found in this season of complete and utter helplessness and how this journey along an unfamiliar path has drawn me deeper into the depths of God's heart. I don't like pain and I don't care for dark, scary places, but God has used both of these to lead me to the treasure trove of blessings that are buried deep within His heart. These treasures are there for anyone who is willing to journey into the unknown and tuck themselves into the very center of His heart.

We are looking forward to enjoying this week before we head to Duke. Mike is feeling strong and we are both "floatin' along" as we rest in God's great river of grace. My prayer for you this morning is that "*out of his glorious riches he may strengthen you with power through his Spirit in your inner being, so that Christ may dwell in your hearts through faith. And I pray that you, being rooted and established in love, may have power, together with all the Lord's holy people, to grasp how wide and long and high and deep is the love of Christ, and to know this love that surpasses knowledge—that you may be filled to the measure of all the fullness of God. Now to him who is able to do immeasurably more than all we ask or imagine, according to his power that is at work within us, to him be glory in the church and in Christ Jesus throughout all generations, for ever and ever! Amen.*" Ephesians 3:16-21

Floatin' along...

# *Finishing Strong...*

Well...Mike will start round 11 of his 12 rounds of treatment tomorrow. In so many ways, it is difficult to believe we are at this point in our journey. On one hand, it seems like we have gotten here at warp speed. On the other hand, this has been the longest year of our lives. We are filled with so many emotions. We are so excited that this leg of the journey is coming to an end. There is a sense of relief and anticipation of life returning to something that resembles "normal". There is a bit of anxiety as we contemplate some important decisions and consider what God's definition of "normal" might look like. There's a sense of awe at what God might have in store, and unfortunately, there is a sense of dread as we consider the many unknowns concerning Mike's long term health.

The past couple of weeks have brought some much needed rest and time to pray and ponder. I'm a bit of a "thinker" and when I have time to be still, I can't help but think...about the past...the present...and the future. I guess I'm just wired that way. My thinking and pondering keeps me grounded and in touch with the Lord. Without time to think, I struggle to have a peaceful, restful heart...all that to say...these past couple of weeks have been long awaited! One of the things that God continues to impress upon my heart is the fact that Mike, the kids, and I (and all who place their faith in Christ) are more than victorious (Romans 8:37)! No matter what battles and trials we face in this life – our victory has already been won and God is calling us to *live* as more than conquerors over our defeated foe! I remember a good friend sharing with me a few years ago what she gleaned about this verse from a book written by John Piper. In the book (sorry, I can't remember which one), Piper explains that in Bible times, when a nation was defeated by their enemy and then returned to do battle with them and won, they would take back all that their enemy had stolen from them in previous battles and distribute the plunder among the citizens of their kingdom and parade their enemy naked through the streets. God wants us to reclaim all that the enemy has stolen from us and use it to build and bless His kingdom. In doing so, we make a spectacle of our enemy, Satan, and his army.

Cancer is definitely a consequence of living in an imperfect, fallen world. Cancer has been our enemy, and I am sure Satan would love to use cancer to steal our joy...our faith...our hope...our passion for following Christ...our dreams for the future...and anything else he can get his grubby, selfish, hands on. Well...too bad! We are more than victorious and we are determined to recapture all that the enemy has stolen from us these past 15 months and use it to bless God's kingdom and bring glory and honor to His name!

Psalm 1 says that when we delight in God's instruction and meditate on it...ponder it...think about it, we will be like a tree, planted by streams of water, that does not wither. I guess being a "thinker" isn't all that bad! My roots run deep into the grace and love of God! When I take time to slow down and think about His goodness and mercy, I feel strong and the scorching sun of life doesn't cause me to wither.

Life is such a gift when we live each day seeking the very heart of God – the One who created our hearts. There is just a sweetness to life regardless of how bitter our circumstances might be. The victory our hearts are longing for has already been won! Will there be more battles – certainly! These are opportunities for us to be MORE than victorious – opportunities to do battle and take back the plunder the enemy has stolen from us and opportunities to bring glory and honor to our King. These are opportunities for us to rise above our circumstances with hope and joy and peace and praise...regardless of how bloody the battle becomes! So much of a life lived like this has to do with choices...choosing to accept suffering and trials...choosing to believe God...choosing to trust God...choosing to fight...choosing to cherish the fact that our true treasure is waiting for us in heaven, not here on earth...choosing to worship the Creator rather than the created...choosing to believe truth rather than lies...TOUGH choices...BEAUTIFUL outcomes!

So...as we move on to the next leg of this journey, we long to turn every painful, dreadful, fearful, difficult moment we have faced into something that shouts the praises of our Lord. We long to share the bounty of His blessings with as many as we can and make His name famous...His touch real...His grace known...His love something others can't live without!

# *Your Story...*

What keeps you "busy"? Is your busyness getting in the way of your desire and ability to be still before the Lord? Our God is not a God of chaos and busyness. He longs for us to prioritize moments in our day to come to Him and sit at His feet. Sometimes we have to come and ask Him to calm our hectic, busy minds. He is patient and He will do just that! It is in these still, quiet moments that we are best able to experience God's love and peace and discern His will for our lives. Take some time today to be still at His feet...even if it means letting some things move to the back burner of your busy, chaotic life! He's waiting! Use the space below to record what the Lord speaks to your heart during these quiet moments...

Chapter Thirteen

# *Looking Back...Pressing on...*

*"But one thing I do: forgetting what is behind and reaching forward to what is ahead, I pursue as my goal the prize promised by God's heavenly call in Christ Jesus. " Philippians 3:13-14 HCSB*

Finding a place to end this book has been difficult. Our journey has yet to come to an end. Although we have been traveling this path for more than a year, in many ways it still feels quite unfamiliar. On the other hand, it feels strangely comfortable and safe. After all, we have become quite content to stay in this place of abiding so deeply in Christ. I suppose in some ways, we dread the thought that this aspect of life might change. Does it have to? Maybe not! I suppose we are the ones to decide. I heard someone say the other day that when the Hebrews would write a story (and maybe they still do), their story has a beginning, a middle, and a beginning. I like that! There is no ending in our life's story, just a series of new beginnings that reflect each chapter in our life. So...there is no ending to this book, but most definitely a beginning to another story!

God calls us to abide in Him...we have free access to His dwelling place...we are the ones that must choose to dwell in the shelter of the Most High (Ps. 91:1). So...that is our plan – to remain tucked into His love...to remain in this place of deep intimate fellowship...to continue resting in His perfect peace...to stubbornly trust Him with every aspect of our lives. He is so deserving of our trust...so worthy of our attention and praise. Although we long to move on to another, less frightening path, we gladly accept the unfamiliar, and we trust fully that our faithful Father will guide us each step of the way. After all, it is the unfamiliar that causes us to focus more intently on each step we take and to be more aware of our surroundings. Our view of life is different now, and that is a blessing in and of itself!

As I consider how to bring this project to a close, I continue to be draw to Paul's words in Philippians 3. He so beautifully paints a picture of what it means to know Christ...truly KNOW Him. Paul's life was forever changed by a close, personal encounter with Christ. From that point on, everything he had gained, he counted as loss compared to KNOWING Christ (Philippians 3:7-8). So, what was Paul's response to this realization? He made KNOWING Christ his determined purpose (v. 13-14). He refused to allow the change in his heart and life to be temporary. Oh, how many times have I done that? How many times have I felt

God's touch on my life only to wander back to the familiar? I long to be like Paul. I long to look back and be inspired to press on! I long for what I see behind me to push me further along my path of pursuing the goal to which God is calling me (v.14).

Did Paul ever look back? I think he did, but not with a longing to go back! No! Paul allowed the past to serve as a constant reminder of how futile life is unless we are following Christ. Paul looked back for a reason...to remind Him of what God had done in his life and to remind himself of how meaningless life is without Christ. No wonder God chose Paul to write most of the New Testament! What an encouragement for us all. We are no different than Paul. God longs to change us in the same way. God longs to capture our hearts the way He captured Paul's. God longs to remove the scales from our eyes so that we can see His glory in a way that would leave us forever changed and forever longing for more of Him and less of this world!

Paul found himself on an unfamiliar path. No longer a Pharisee, Paul was called to share the gospel with those he once persecuted. Now, I call that an unfamiliar path! He was the one being persecuted and thrown into prison. I mean, can you imagine the change in Paul's circumstances? Only a change in heart can explain Paul's response. Regardless of his circumstances, he was committed to the "call". He fully trusted that God would supply all his needs (Philippians 4:19). Everything that Paul once considered of great worth he now saw as rubbish...trash...a waste of time...compared to the worth of knowing Christ, his Lord and Savior. WOW...to have that kind of faith and commitment to Christ!

So, here we are, coming to the end of this leg of our journey with cancer. Mike will soon finish his clinical trial at Duke. What is next...we have no idea! All we know is that God is for us and He is in control...still on His throne...still loving us...still providing for us...still calling us to follow Him along this unfamiliar path. That is our plan...to follow Him. Wherever He leads, we will follow. If we have learned anything along this journey it is that following God into the unknown is far safer than blazing our own trail! The cliché is true – the safest place to be is in the eye of the storm. It is true physically and spiritually! The safest place to be when the storms of life come is tucked into the heart of God – in the very center of His will. After all, that is where His will is determined – in His heart...a heart that is full of love for us!

I feel like God is calling me to end this book before the journey is finished. In my mind, I had planned on writing until we finished the clinical trial at Duke. That would have been a nice place to wrap this up. It would have felt complete. It would have felt right – to me at least! God had a different plan. I'm not sure why, but I suspect that it has something to do with the fact that this journey is not over (inject a tone of sarcastic humor here). Truth is...the journey is never over until we are made complete in Him ...fully transformed into His image...forever abiding in Him.

And so...our journey continues...unfamiliar as it may be...we are pressing on towards to goal...the prize...waiting for us in heaven!

# *Your Story...*

Take some time to think about the many ways God has touched your life.  Can you say, without a doubt and with full sincerity that you count everything as loss compared to knowing Christ? That is God's desire for all of us.  It is truly the ultimate goal and necessity of living the crucified life.  Unless we can echo Paul's words with 100% sincerity, we are likely to live as an enemy of the cross...full of pride and selfishness...focused on worldly things rather than on eternal things (Philippians 3:18-19). The choice is ours and our enemy would love for us to believe that there is more satisfaction in living for ourselves and our own desires rather than for the kingdom of God.  Even in suffering, we are to live for Christ.  We can conquer the sting of suffering and even physical death by believing, with all our hearts, that there is eternal PURPOSE in our pain.  Use this time to pour out your heart to Him.  You may be in a place of pain right now, or you may know a loved one who is suffering.  Maybe you just happened to pick up this book or received it from someone you know.  If so, it was not by accident.  God is calling you to a deeper place of KNOWING Him.  He is a God of purpose and His desire is to be a part of your life...to be the very breath of your life.  He is waiting to meet with you right now!  Will you respond? I am praying right now that you will!

**Chapter Fourteen**

## *Surrender...*

*"Father, if you are willing, remove this cup from me. Nevertheless, not my will, but Yours, be done" Psalm 27:14 ESV*

As you might have discovered by reading the last chapter, I had planned to end this memoire and collection of journal entries at the point that Mike finished his clinical trial treatment at Duke University. There were a couple of reasons for this decision. First, we were ready to launch the Isiah 42:16 ministry and wanted to have the book published and ready to sell as a means to raise funds for the ministry. Secondly, because it seemed like a perfect "ending." However, that is nowhere near where our journey and story ends and there is so much more to tell and share about the greatness of God and the hope, comfort and blessings we continued to experience along this unfamiliar path. So, I decided to do a revised edition of the book to share "the rest of the story".

Although this chapter of our story did not end in the way we had hoped it would, it ended well! Between the beginning and the end of this chapter in our lives, there were thousands of moments where we experienced and were sustained by the grace of God in ways that left us more and more in awe of Him and confident in His faithfulness to guide us, provide for us, heal our hearts, and fill our hearts with unshakable faith, hope and joy despite the pain we endured. In case you are new to our story, Mike went home to spend eternity with Jesus on December 17, 2013. I wish I had space in this book to share details about this leg of the journey. In all honestly, this leg of the journey warrants a book all its own, but I have decided not to tackle that endeavor at this time. I do, however, hope I can share glimpses into this season that will in some way help, comfort, encourage or inspire you. More than anything, I hope this revision will accurately portrait and bring to life the realities of what it looks like to rest in the refuge of God during times of suffering, hardship, and trials despite the emotions and heartache and fear. I hope our story will somehow help others to walk along these unfamiliar paths with confidence that He is walking with us, making the rough places smooth and faithful to never leave us or forsake us! So...here it is...the rest of the story...

## Catching Our Breath...

Mike finished up his clinical trial at the end of the summer in 2011. The clinical trial was a year of oral chemo and monthly transfusions along with frequent trips to the Duke University brain tumor center as well as visits with his local oncologist. He tolerated treatment incredibly well and we continued to receive the glorious news of clear MRIs. Thank you Jesus!!! At the end of his clinical trial he was feeling strong and his quality of life was amazing and beyond what we had ever imagined. While on disability, he assumed the role of stay-at-home dad. He loved and cherished every moment of carting the kids to and from school activities, orthodontist appointments, taking them and their friends to Dollywood, cooking and even cleaning! He was Mr. Mom to the max! Shortly after he finished his treatments, we received an incredible surprise blessing from a dear friend. She had signed up to run a marathon at Disney World. On the day she ran the race, a package was delivered to our house. In the package was a ragged pair of her running shoes she had worn while training for the marathon. The shoes were stuffed full of money. *WHAT IN THE WORLD?*, we thought. We opened the card that accompanied the extravagant (and peculiar) contents of the package. In the card, she explained that while she was training for her marathon she often became discouraged and was tempted to quit and give up. She would often train by running the loop at Cades Cove in the Smoky Mountains. On one occasion, she was about half way around the loop and ready to quit...like to the point of tears ready to quit!...then she thought of Mike and the incredible marathon he was "running" in his battle against cancer. She thought about his tenacity, positive attitude, and "never give up" spirit. Inspired by Mike's journey, she pressed on with a renewed determination to not allow her physical and mental exhaustion to get the best of her. Thankful for his inspiration, she decided to secretly invite people in our church to sponsor her run and raise money to bless our family. We were floored! I'll just say...it took us a while to count all those bills! It was an overwhelming gesture of love!

We decided we would use the money raised by our friend to take a much needed family vacation. In June of 2012, we enjoyed a two week wild west adventure that took us through southern Utah, the Grand Canyon, Colorado, up to Yellow Stone National Park and over to the Grand Teton Mountains in Wyoming. Roughly a 3,000 mile trek filled with laughter, breath taking scenery, stinky teenage feet and other stinky teenage boy problems, multiple stops at ice cream shops, and pure joy! Mike was feeling so strong and I am not exaggerating when I say he out-hiked us all! It was such a gift to our family to have this time together. Over the next few months, Mike continued to undergo monthly MRIs and we received reports of no tumor growth. Although we were rejoicing in these good reports and beginning to breathe a little more easily, we were still clinging tight to hope and looking to God to protect our hearts and minds from worry, enabling us to fully experience the joy that came with the words, "Your MRI looks beautiful." However, on the other hand, we also felt a continued urgency to pray without ceasing and seek His face like never before.

In looking back at my journals, I think the thing the Lord was teaching me most in this season is the importance of not only seeking Him and drawing close to Him in times of crisis or need, but to seek Him and abide on a daily basis regardless of how calm and "easy" life is. Ease and the perception of predictability can be such enemies to our intimacy with God and dependence on Him. We can so easily become self-reliant and drift into a pattern of only coming to God when we feel overwhelmed or face a need or trial that we just can't seem to handle on our own (news flash...we are never meant to handle life on our own!). So much of our attention seems to be focused on the temporal realities of this life. We can become so distracted by the material things and pleasures of this world that we gradually and unnoticeably slip into the trap of living for this world and for our own comfort. We convince ourselves that we love Jesus, but what we really love is this world and all that we can squeeze out of it for our good and our pleasure. Jesus reminds us in Matthew 6 that where our treasure is...our hearts will follow. This journey has been such a blessing in that our suffering led us to abide in a way that helped us see more clearly the treasure that Jesus truly is, and it has helped us to see the reality of our self-reliance and love of worldly comforts that have stolen far too much of our attention. The things of this life are temporary, but our relationship with Jesus is eternal. Paul talks about this in 2 Corinthians 4. The things and pleasures and sufferings of this world are temporary, but the things that are unseen...the spiritual blessings of knowing Jesus, are eternal and they are our greatest gift and treasure. So...in the good times and in the hard times, when we look to Jesus to satisfy our every need and desire, we will experience the fullness of His love and grace and blessings rather than seek and settle for the worthless treasures of this world!

## From The Mountain To The Valleys...

We all love those mountain top experiences where it is easy to trust God...easy to praise Him...easy to trace His hand...easy to see His grace being poured out. But...what about those times when we are face down in the muck and mire of life? Times when we find ourselves hemmed in by the dark clouds that accompany trials and suffering. Times when our dreams seem to be shattered into dust or every emotion and thought seems contrary to what we know to be true and there is an intense internal battle going on in our hearts. What then? I believe the answer to those questions depends on the condition of our heart before the battle even begins and before we are thrust into the valley where doubt and anger and fear and confusion lie lurking in the shadows ready to take us captive. When the heart is prepared for battle, we will respond in faith. When the heart is prepared for battle we will do what we are accustomed to doing...we will trust God...seek His face...and ask that His will be done!

Towards the middle of November 2012, we were drop kicked off our mountain top by the news that Mike's cancer had returned. This news was such a disappointment for us to say the least! We had just gotten to a place where we were comfortable thinking and dreaming about the future...more than just a month or so at a time...but really dreaming long term. We were praying and asking God to give us some direction and insight into where He was leading our family in terms of ministry and life in general. We were praying and asking God to confirm whether our dreams were in line with His plans. Now, we have had to hit the pause button...or maybe the rewind button....or maybe this was our answer. In reality, we all have to dare to dream with a willingness to lay OUR dreams on the altar for the sake of allowing God's plans and His will to shape and define our dreams just like Abraham laid his son on the altar of sacrifice, trusting that the Lord would be faithful to keep the promises He had already made. If we are not willing to do that, we run the risk of doubting what we know to be true and questioning God's faithfulness thus slipping into all kinds of pits and snares that the enemy longs to drag us into.

So, in this moment of tumbling head first off the mountain and into the valley, we chose to believe that He had plans for us...plans for a hope and a future...plans to prosper us and not harm us (Jeremiah 29:11). We allowed Proverbs 3:5-6 to guide us each step of the way...leaning NOT on our own understanding but seeking His wisdom...knowing He would direct our path, guard our hearts, and provide the grace we needed to continue along this unfamiliar path. He is the One who makes all things possible. He makes healing possible...He makes surviving grief possible...He makes ALL things possible so that His will can be done. The only question was would we have hearts that were surrendered to HIS will? I've never believed in a name it and claim it theology. To be frank...I think that is a selfish theology that is often times more concerned with our good that God's will. Do I believe God could have healed Mike...ABSOLUTELY!!!!! Did I believe God WOULD heal Mike...absolutely IF it accomplished His will and brought the most glory to His name. Did I pray for healing...YES! Was healing here on this earth the ONLY outcome we hoped for...not necessarily. People are often shocked when I share this, but it is absolutely true. We genuinely wanted nothing more than God's will, and our number one desire was for God to be glorified in whatever way He chose. That was and still is a hard pill to swallow and a difficult level of surrender to achieve. We were only able to genuinely desire this by the grace of God. We reminded ourselves daily that our lives are not our own, but we have been bought at a price (1 Corinthians 6:19-20)...that God was working these struggles together for our good (Romans 8:28)...that His ways are perfect even though they are often impossible to understand and comprehend (Deuteronomy 32:4).

Though we were devastated by the news that his cancer was back, we could see God's sovereign hand at work. Mike had been experiencing some headaches so his oncologist in Knoxville ordered an MRI. He was not suppose to have another regularly scheduled MRI for several more weeks. Had he waited until his next MRI, these new tumors would have progressed in severity and the disease would have been much more advanced and difficult to treat. In December, he underwent a procedure where they use very high powered, laser focused radiation to zap the tumors (there were three) and he was put back on a treatment protocol of two types of chemo and avastin infusions. Unfortunately, doctors were left with using less effective treatment protocols than what he had received in the clinical trial. The medications would also have more severe side effects. In February, we made a trip to Duke and the MRI showed that the radio surgery and new protocol were working and there were no signs of the three tumors that were zapped or any new tumors. Unfortunately, we were dealt another blow when we talked to the doctor at Duke. She seemed particularly interested in Mike's quality of life since starting the new treatment protocol. She was concerned that he experience the highest quality of life possible given that "things could change quickly" (code words for...this cancer is relentless and your next MRI may not look as good). She anticipated one of two scenarios...either he would stay on this protocol for a year and the cancer would stay at bay OR we would see the cancer become resistant to the treatment and see progression of the disease in approximately 6 months. The odds were stacked against him given that his reoccurrence was multifocal and had managed to "travel around and effect multiple parts of the brain". Talk about a gut punch! We continued to rest in the peace that God promises to give when we place our lives in

His hands and trust Him with all our hearts. Easier said than done sometimes, but not because of His lack of faithfulness but ours! As Mike and I talked on the ride home, we both agreed that God was continuing to teach us about surrender on this leg of the journey and to live life to the fullest for His glory.

So here is a recap...mid November, three new tumors were identified on Mike's MRI. Mike started a new treatment protocol and the tumors were zapped in December with a radiation procedure called radiosurgery. The radiation seemed to have "killed" the tumors. The doctors were cautiously optimistic, but we all new unless God intervened with a miracle, we were no longer on the offense. The cancer had the advantage now and we were playing hardball defense to try and stop the progression of the disease. Given that the cancer had migrated to different parts of the brain left doctors gently bringing us into the reality of what the future might hold. By April, another MRI revealed further progression, which required another change in treatment protocol. Once the cancer becomes resistant to the current treatment, the only choice is to try something different. Unfortunately, each change comes with diminished effectiveness and more severe side effects. We saw the intensity of his side effects increase almost instantly. Over the next few months, the prognosis became more and more grim. More progression of the disease, another change in chemo, which in turn brought about more severe symptoms and poorer quality of life. Through it all, Mike continued to teach us all so much about giving thanks in all things, remaining steadfast in faith when faced with the darkest of circumstances, an smiling even when you don't have much to smile about by the worlds standards. We did not talk much about the reality that his life on this earth was soon coming to an end. Instead, we made the most of each day and celebrated the goodness of God.

Now...I don't want to give you the impression that everything was rosy and that we skipped through each day sprinkling Jesus everywhere we went. There were some tough days! Day's we had to wrestle and fight with our flesh and selfishness. Days we had some pretty ugly pity parties and days we felt defeated and scared. Here is one of my journal entries I would like to share from back in June 2013, when things were really beginning to be difficult and daunting and downright frightening.

### Raw...real...a little ugly... — Jun 30, 2013

> *Most of the time my posts are written on the side of victory rather than in the midst of or through the battle. Today...I am writing in the midst of the battle. I know that there are many of you who are in the midst of a trial right now and I want to share the real...raw...and little bit ugly side of walking this journey. Number one...I want you to know you are not alone. Number two...well...I just feel led to.*
>
> *This past week has been incredibly difficult. We have felt hard pressed...but not crushed praise the Lord. This morning's message at church reminded me that God uses the trials and tribulations of life to press us and squeeze out the dross and sift out the chaff that is keeping us from His transformation process of making us more and more like Christ. So...we need to not wiggle and squirm our way out from underneath the pressure, but rather hold up under it and allow it to accomplish God's will and purpose. I was just thinking yesterday about how I need NOT pray for LESS of the pressure/trial and pray for MORE of His grace. My natural human, fleshly prayer is for God to remove what is squeezing me...if I am truly praying in the Spirit, I should be praying that God would give me the grace to persevere and trust that this pressure and squeezing is for my good. BUT...this week the pressure has been extra heavy and painful. The pressure is bringing....*

**PAIN**...*as I watch Mike struggle and wrestle with changes and physical and emotional turmoil. LORD, USE THIS PAIN TO DEVELOP COMPASSION IN MY HEART FOR THOSE WHO HURT*

**GRIEF**...*grief is a response to loss. I am grieving what we have lost in terms of health and our old life and I am grieving the thought of what I might still lose. LORD HELP ME TO REMEMBER THAT EVERYTHING IS RUBISH COMPARED TO KNOWING JESUS...HELP ME TO COUNT ALL AS A LOSS COMPARED TO KNOWING YOU.*

**LONLINESS**...*Not so much physical loneliness...but emotional loneliness because it is difficult to share with others who can truly relate. THANK YOU LORD THAT YOU CAN RELATE AND LONG TO SPEAK TRUTH INTO MY HEART AND PEACE INTOMY SOUL*

**SADNESS**...*This week, the depth of sadness I have felt has been overwhelming. Sadness when I think about losing Mike...sadness when I think about the kids losing their dad...sadness when I think about what this must be like for Mike...sadness for his parents and family members. LORD, THANK YOU THAT YOU TOOK MY PAIN AND MY SORROWS AND MADE THEM YOUR VERY OWN. OH HOW MARVELOUS, OH HOW WONDERFUL IS MY SAVIOR'S LOVE FOR ME*

**FRUSTRATION**...*I feel helpless. I want answers and assurance, but I know this is not what my heart needs!!! I need FAITH!!!! THANK YOU LORD THAT YOU GIVE WISDOM GENEROUSLY WHEN I ASK...HELP MY SOUL TO NOT BE TOSSED TO AND FRO ON THE WAVES OF DOUBT.*

*HELP MY PEACE AND HOPE TO BE FOUND IN YOU...NOT
MY CIRCUMSTANCES OR MEDICAL ANSWERS AND
ASSURANCE OF EASE.*

*As I honestly come before the throne of grace, I asking
the Lord to help me to BE STILL under the pressure of this
trial and fully surrendered rather than wiggling and
squirming my way out. The pressure is great and it hurts!
In my flesh...I want out! In the Spirit...I want to endure
and for God to accomplish His will and purpose. I think
sometimes, we want God to transform us by hanging
trinkets and ornaments on us that reflect His glory rather
than cutting away and pruning the things that do not.
That is not God's way of transforming us...by just
"dressing us up a bit." God's Word is a double edge sword
He uses to cut away our flesh and anything that does not
reflect His glory. Trees bear fruit as the result of what is
going on inside the tree. Fruit is not placed on the tree.*

*So...today...my prayer is LORD SQUEEZE ME...PRUNE
ME...BRING THE DROSS TO THE SURFACE...PRESS ME
AND SIFT ME OF THE CHAFF AND BURN IT UP...GIVE ME
GRACE TO BE STILL AND BEAR UP UNDER THIS
PRESSURE...LORD...MAY YOUR GLORY BE MANIFESTED
THROUGH THIS TRIAL!!!!*

*Where the Spirit of the Lord is, there is freedom!!! Even
under the pressure of tribulation, peace and hope and
freedom can be found when we surrender our hearts to
the Word and will of God!!!*

Over the next few months, Mike's symptoms continued to
worsen and his quality of life and functioning continued to deteriorate
rather rapidly. By the end of summer, he was no longer able to drive and

need someone to be with him 24/7. There were many moments of sleeplessness for me. In those moments of sleeplessness, God was teaching me that the greatest way to demonstrate my trust in Him is to just simply sit quietly in His presence and listen to Him sing over me. I don't need to say anything...I don't need the "right words"...I don't need to speak...I just need to BE STILL!!!!

In that day it will be said to Jerusalem:
"Do not be afraid, O Zion;
Do not let your hands fall limp.
"The Lord your God is in your midst,
A victorious warrior.
He will exult over you with joy,
He will be quiet in His love,
He will rejoice over you with shouts of joy. (Zeph 3:17)

His songs quieted me with His love and reminded me that HE IS A VICTORIOUS WARRIOR who FIGHTS FOR ME AND MY FAMILY!!!! And though my hands felt worn out and tired...they did not grow limp but I continued to raise them in praise and adoration to the One who sings over and fights for my family in the midst of this horrible trial! HE HAS brought victory on so many levels!!!! The greatest victory is already won! We are forever His children! Other victories were won as well...my children saw God's hand at work and their faith grew as a result of this trial! All of God's promises are YES because of Jesus. So I know something beautiful will come from these ashes. I already see it happening. God is so faithful to fulfill His promises when we believe them and seek Him! Thank Him for that today...listen to Him sing over you!!!!

## *Sailing Home...*

August 30, 2013 is a day I will never forget. It is etched in my mind, or should I say seared in my mind by the intense pain and anguish it held. Each detail in vivid HD color. After a heart-to-heart talk with our friend and practitioner Shanda, we all agreed that it was time to terminate treatment. The side effects of the drugs were diminishing Mike's quality of life, the tumors were continuing to grow and spread, and we could no longer ignore the reality. The Lord was calling Him home.

After sharing the news with the kids together as a family, Mike spent some one-on-one time with each of them. Still to this day, I have no idea what was said. It was a sacred moment for each of them and one I hope changed them forever and still resonates in their hearts. Their dad taught them so much about living while fighting to live. While dying, he taught them so much about living and what is truly important in life. He taught them that his relationship with Jesus was the most important thing in his life. He modeled for them what it means to take up your cross and follow Christ. He taught them what true servant leadership looks like. He showed them how to genuinely worship and praise the Lord for who He is. He displayed peace that surpasses all understanding, which was the result of deep abiding. Could he have taught his kids these things without going through this trial? Maybe. But this is the way God chose for him, and he made it very clear to his kids that he understood that and had accepted God's will for his life.

In October of 2013, we were blessed with another amazing opportunity to get away as a family to one of our favorite places...Destin. Mike had really begun to show significant decline in the weeks before our trip, but he suddenly rebounded just days before our trip and we had the most amazing time full of sweet moments we all still cherish in our hearts today. The day we left Destin to come home, he began having headaches. By Thanksgiving, he was using a walker, on oxygen and experiencing some significant cognitive and physical changes. I knew we had some rough days ahead so my prayers became focused on begging

God to be merciful to Mike and my kids. I prayed that his last days would be peaceful, calm, and seasoned with God's goodness and grace. The Lord answered these prayers in ways that were exceedingly and abundantly beyond what we could have thought to ask or imagine. Mike passed peacefully in the quiet of the wee hours of the morning in our home. I thank God for his grace in that moment and in the days leading up to his home going. It could have been much more traumatic for my kids, but God, in His loving kindness, consumed our home with a peace and calmness that truly surpasses explanation. The day before Mike went home, I wrote him this poem and read it to him. I hold on to the hope that, although he was unresponsive, he was able to hear my words and look forward to the journey he was about to embark on as he set sail for heaven. Mike loved to sail! Every summer, we would visit his parents at their lake home in Indiana. It is a special place to us and we cherish all the memories of our time spent there each summer. One of the things Mike look forward to most on our visits was being able to sail. I know the Lord gave me these words to comfort both of us as we said good-bye...

*Sail away to heavens shores*
*Where pain and sickness are no more*
*Your Savior waits to welcome you home*
*Your place reserved before God's throne*
*With all the angels and saints you will sing*
*Forever hallelujahs to your King*
*Your praises will not end*
*His glory bright and true*
*No longer veiled from your view*
*Grace so perfect, love so pure*
*Perfect worship; Your hearts desire*
*Sail away on your voyage home*
*Your journey has come to an end*
*Your treasures you will lay at His feet*
*From a life so full and complete*
*We will miss you*
*You can't be replaced*
*Sail away home now...*
*You've sailed a great race!!!*

It is hard to comprehend in our human finite minds why God allows His children to suffer. We just have to filter every question through the truth that God is good and He loves us and created us for His glory. It is there within those truths that we find the divine answers to our hard questions. They cannot be answered in the human realm! What grater love is there than when a man lays down his life for a friend. I feel like Mike has done that...surrendered his life here on this earth for the good of others and of course ultimately for God's glory. Everything that God allows ultimately has the potential to glorify Himself...the question is WILL WE? Will we surrender our hopes and dreams and desires and even our life in order to glorify Him. Will we trust that God can and will allow hardships and suffering for His glory and for our good...that those two things can be accomplished simultaneously even through the hardest of circumstances? I guess they really aren't two mutually exclusive events...when God is glorified in our lives it is for our good. The glory must always be first...our good is a natural, automatic consequence but HIS GLORY is the ultimate priority...not our good. When Jesus went into the garden to pray the night before His crucifixion, He began his prayer with these words, *"Father the hour has come, glorify your Son so that the Son may glorify You...I have glorified You on earth by completing the work You gave me to do. Now, Father, glorify Me in Your presence with that glory I had with You before the world existed."* (John 17:1; 4-5; HCSB). In Luke 22:42, we see the heart of Jesus summed up in these words, *"Father, if you are willing, remove this cup from me. Nevertheless, not my will, but Yours, be done"* (Psalm 27:14 ESV). Only the power of the Holy Spirit can give us strength to pray these words and surrender completely to the will of God in moments of suffering. I can also say with confidence that genuinely praying these words does not free us from the pain and anguish we feel, but praying these words will bring an outpouring of peace that will comfort our hearts and give us confidence and joy in knowing that our suffering has a purpose and, ultimately, will glorify God.

I long to give away what God has poured into our lives these past 9 years as we've navigated our way this journey. Oh how I desperately want others to experience the depths of His love and grace and mercy and goodness like we have. I know it is His desire for ALL to see Him for who He really is...to see Him in a way that leaves us hungry and thirsty for more. Like David in the sanctuary saying...I have beheld your glory...your love is better than life! There's truly no better place to be than in a place of complete and total surrender to the will of God. Getting there isn't easy, and it is IMPOSSIBLE in our own strength. It requires the help of the Holy Spirit and a heart that is daily surrendered and willing to say, not my will but Yours, Lord. But, this place of surrender is the most peaceful and freeing place I have every been and I consider the journey to get here a blessing and one of most fruitful journeys in my walk with Jesus.

# *Your Story...*

Take some time to consider any areas of your life that may not be surrendered to God's will. Your career? Your children? Your marriage? Your finances? Your health? I have found from experience that when areas of my life are not fully surrendered to the Lord, I often experience anxiety and struggle with trying to control these areas in a way that prevents struggle and hardship when things don't go my way. Often times, areas of life that are not surrendered are characterized by fear and preoccupation of our thoughts. As you take an inventory of the areas of your life looking for ways God may be calling you to surrender, be on the lookout for things that may be consuming your thought life, causing you to experience fear and anxiety. It is not always a comfortable process, but I can promise you it will be a process that will bear much fruit and develop a deeper intimacy with Jesus and a greater understanding of God's character and will for your life!

**Chapter 15**

# Held...Hidden...Healed

*"fear not, for I am with you; be not dismayed, for I am your God; I will strengthen you, I will help you, I will uphold you with my righteous right hand."* (Isaiah 41:10; ESV)

# *Held...*

Losing Mike was an incredibly crushing experience. The grief
was so heavy it literally felt as if I was suffocating. I found it difficult to
even breathe let alone function and think and plan. I remember lying in
bed one night and feeling an intense pain in my chest. It was as if I could
literally feel my heart breaking. God reminded me of the true meaning
of a covenant relationship...two become one. I realized that my heart
was no longer whole and when Mike went home, there was a tearing
away of our two hearts that had been joined together over twenty years
ago. I knew in that moment, that there was nothing I could do to escape
the pain, go around the pain, or avoid the pain. I knew I had to go
through it, and I knew my faithful covenant keeping God would be with
me. One of my all-time favorite books of the Bible is Isaiah. It gives us
such a glimpse into the heart of our covenant keeping God. In Isaiah 43,
we read this beautiful promise that God made to Israel and I believe, as
His child, it is a promise He has made to me and all His children.

*"Now this is what the LORD says – the One who created Jacob, and the One
who formed you, Israel – Do not fear, for I have redeemed you; I have called
you by your name; you are Mine. I will be with you when you pass through
the waters, and when you pass through the rives, they will not overwhelm
you. You will not be scorched when you walk through the fire, and the flame
will not burn you. " (HCSB)*

For me, losing Mike was like being shoved off the safe, lush,
relaxing, tranquil bank of a river. The grief journey has been like
struggling for dear life in the midst of this raging river...trying to stay
afloat...at times tossed and turned and taken under by swift
rapids...unable to find anything to grab hold of and always floating down
stream away from where I had been and longed to be...desperately
wanting to reach the other side and find safety (knowing I could never
"go back" to the side I had once been on)...worn out from fighting the
undertow of grief and constant struggle. At times, I didn't really care

where I landed...I just wanted the struggle to survive to end! I am finally in a place where I can say I have reached the other side. I still look back, often with a deep sense of longing for what once was, but for the most part I look forward with great confidence and anticipation that what is ahead is full of goodness and blessings and joy. What is ahead will never be "what was", but I know it will be exactly what the Lord has planned. If I continue to seek Him and trust Him ,I will end up exactly where I am suppose to be. When I share my story with people who are in the raging river stage of grief, they often ask, "how did you get through the pain...doubt...anger...fear about the future...etc." I have thought a lot about how to answer that question. I have even asked myself that question. Though there were many practical ways I survived day to day and struggle by struggle, I believe the one thing that kept me from drowning in that raging river of grief is this...I KNOW GOD!!!

I **KNOW** Him! Even in the darkest most painful moments, I KNEW without a single doubt that He could be trusted and that He was sovereign and in control and working for my good. I guess you could say that my trust and confidence in Him was my life preserver that kept me from drowning in that turbulent river of grief. Even in the moments when I couldn't see or feel anything changing or any signs that I would reach the other side...I KNEW I would because I KNOW His true character. I KNEW He heard my prayers...I KNEW He saw my tears...I KNEW He felt my pain. I NEVER doubted His goodness and love for me. I KNEW He would provide the grace I needed to make it through each day (especially the darkest days that I felt would consume me). That is what kept me afloat...that is what gave me hope...that is what healed my heart...KNOWING HIM...KNOWING I could trust Him...KNOWING He was working for me and in me...KNOWING He would redeem my brokenness...KNOWING He would pull me out of the pit and give me a new song, a hymn of praise...KNOWING He would allow every struggle to somehow display His glory...KNOWING I am more than victorious through Christ...KNOWING HIM has gotten me through! I knew without a doubt that I was held in His firm grip and held within the refuge of His loving arms. There were so many things I did not know, but I KNEW He is who He says He is without one single shred of doubt. Knowing God is so vital to surviving the pain and hardships of this life.

## Hidden...

When I decided to revise this manuscript, I went back through my caringbridge journals in an effort to somehow summarize the past five years since Mike left us into something meaningful. I had no idea where to begin. So much time has passed and we have seen God work in so many ways. He has gone before us each step of the way. He has held us when we didn't have the strength to hold on. He has tenderly and patiently cleaned out the shrapnel left behind in our hearts. Grief is such a blinding experience. It completely obstructs your view of life and ability to see even the next step. But, when we place our faith and trust in the sovereign Lord of this universe, He is faithful to lead us and keep us from tumbling into despair. There's a difference between grief and despair. Despair is void of hope. When we place our faith and trust in God, even though we are blinded by grief, there is always a glimmer of hope; a tiny glow beyond the fog. Over time, the fog of grief that blinds us begins to thin out and the glimmer of hope shines brighter and brighter. Soon, we break through the fog and find we are able to grieve with a clear view of the goodness that lies ahead and the work that He did in the darkest seasons of our grief. The tiny glimmer becomes a full blown beacon that constantly reminds us that the Lord is near to the broken hearted...He cares for the widows and orphans...He heals our broken hearts...He is our refuge in times of trouble...He is Jehovah Jireh, our provider...He is Jehovah Rapha, the Lord who heals...He works all things together for our good...His grace will sustain us...His strength is made perfect in our weakness...His love is limitless...He is the lifter of our heads when we don't have the strength to look up...HE IS EVERYTHING WE NEED and HE IS ENOUGH!

I wish I could say that fixing my eyes on Jesus has been easy on this journey, but I am sure you would see right through that lie! At times

250

it has been easy, but most of the time, it has been an all-out battle! At times, it literally felt like the devil had his hands around my ankles trying to drag me into a pit of despair. At times, I was almost convinced it would just be easier to jump into the pit of despair and give up fighting. At times I was just flat out numb and the fog of grief would roll back in and the beacon of hope was once again a tiny glimmer. Nevertheless, regardless of my wavering, God remained constant and faithful! That is one of the greatest lessons I have learned on this journey...regardless of our wandering and doubts and refusal to seek His face...HE IS CONSTANT!!! He never changes and His promises are true regardless of how difficult they are to believe.

I remember the day we received the pathology report like it was yesterday. I needed a place to be alone. I went into my closet and closed the door. There, in the darkness and stillness, I begged God to speak and tell me this was all going to be ok. In that moment, the Holy Spirit brought to mind Matthew 11. John the Baptist is in prison and about to be beheaded. In this moment of suffering and I am sure overwhelmed by emotions, John has a crisis of faith. John the Baptist...the one who leapt in his mother's womb when Mary, pregnant with Jesus, came into the room. John the Baptist...the one chosen to usher in the kingdom of heaven. John the Baptist, who recognized the Messiah while he was in the womb, now in the midst of a crisis needed assurance that despite his emotions he could trust what he knew to be true. In that moment, I wasn't quite sure what the Holy Spirit was trying to tell me. I felt like His message was communicating one of two things. Was He simply reminding me to trust what I knew to be true despite the tsunami of emotions that were overcoming my heart, or was He letting me know (like John the Baptist) that the outcome was not going to be what I had hoped and, despite this journey ending in death, I needed to walk in confidence that Jesus is who He says He is and all His promises remain true despite the suffering we were about to experience. WOW! I wasn't quite sure what to do with this message from the Lord, but I knew He was reminding me that He is still the One who speaks and quiets the storm. He is still the One who heals for the glory of God. He is still the

251

One who comforts us in our times of suffering and grief. He is still who He says He is! Although I was uncertain about exactly what the Holy Spirit was trying to tell me by bringing this passage of scripture to mind, it brought me great comfort! He met me there and He spoke to my heart! For the time being...that was enough! I wish I could share all the many ways the Lord has met me personally along this journey since Mike went home. That would be a book in and of itself. If you are traveling the unfamiliar path of grief of widowhood and want to read more about my journey, you can still access our Caringbridge page at https://www.caringbridge.org/visit/mikehearn1/journal or you can also read some of the lessons I have learned on my blog Lessons Lived by going to https://loriuhearn.wordpress.com.

Some of the biggest challenges and most difficult aspects of my grief and journey into widowhood have simultaneously been some of the greatest teachable moments and opportunities for growth in my relationship with Jesus and my confidence in Him. I know everyone's experience with grief and losing a spouse is different, but I also believe there are a few struggles and aspects of this type of journey that are universal although they may look different in how they play out. My biggest struggle has been the feeling of loneliness and isolation. You don't have to be alone to feel lonely and isolated. Even when surrounded by friends and family, I still felt a lone. It was a loneliness that came from the reality that most could not understand what I was going through. Over the years, I've come to refer to this as a season of being held, hidden and healed. Hidden in the sense that I felt alone and held in the sense that in my hiddenness, the Lord was holding me close to His heart in a secret place...a place that was a refuge offering moments of deep intimacy with the Lord that were needed and necessary for healing to take place. As I have reflected over the past 5 years, I have come to the realization that this season of hiddenness had great purpose. God used this season of isolation (both physically and emotionally) to draw me deeper and deeper into His heart. There were many moments when only the Lord saw and understood the depths of my grief and pain, partly because I hid it from others and partly because others just did not see. At first, I fought it. I felt forgotten. I battled resentment and felt hurt that others didn't notice or if they did, they did not reach out. I threw some amazing pity parties lol! Jesus usually didn't show up for those, but instead He patiently waited for me to get over myself and look up! Like a parent who watches patiently while their toddler is thrashing about in a fit of frenzy, the Lord waited and when I was "done", He sat me in His lap and tended to my hurting, frustrated, scared heart. Five years down the road, there is still a measure of this hiddenness that defines my days, but I view it and respond to it differently. I am learning to embrace it with hopes of reaping everything the Lord intends to accomplish in it. I am learning to be still and wait upon the Lord. Psalm 27 is one of the passages of scripture that resonates with me and helps me express what this season of hiddenness is like. I've highlighted a few verses that have been etched in my heart.

# Psalm 27

**The LORD is my light and my salvation—**
**whom shall I fear?**
**The LORD is the stronghold of my life—**
**of whom shall I be afraid?**
*When the wicked advance against me*
*to devour me,*
*it is my enemies and my foes*
*who will stumble and fall.*
*Though an army besiege me,*
*my heart will not fear;*
*though war break out against me,*
*even then I will be confident.*
**One thing I ask from the LORD,**
**this only do I seek:**

*that I may dwell in the house of the LORD
all the days of my life,
to gaze on the beauty of the LORD
and to seek him in his temple.
For in the day of trouble
he will keep me safe in his dwelling;
he will hide me in the shelter of his sacred tent
and set me high upon a rock.
Then my head will be exalted
above the enemies who surround me;
at his sacred tent I will sacrifice with shouts of joy;
I will sing and make music to the LORD.
Hear my voice when I call, LORD;
be merciful to me and answer me.
My heart says of you, "Seek his face!"
Your face, LORD, I will seek.
Do not hide your face from me,
do not turn your servant away in anger;
you have been my helper.
Do not reject me or forsake me,
God my Savior.
Though my father and mother forsake me,
the LORD will receive me.
Teach me your way, LORD;
lead me in a straight path
because of my oppressors.
Do not turn me over to the desire of my foes,
for false witnesses rise up against me,
spouting malicious accusations.
I remain confident of this:
I will see the goodness of the LORD
in the land of the living.
Wait for the LORD;*

*be strong and take heart*
*and wait for the LORD. (ESV)*

The Lord is truly a dwelling place in times of trouble! When we dwell in the refuge of His love, it can oftentimes feel very isolating from a human standpoint. This nearness and intimacy is often directly tied to circumstances that others cannot fully comprehend. Sadly, we can often grow accustomed to and even favor the comfort and intimacy with others more than we value comfort and intimacy we receive when we dwell in the secret place of being hidden in Him. Spending time in these hidden places enables us to gaze upon His beauty...to see and be changed by His glory. Beholding His glory is such a gift that develops in us a longing to be in His presence. Read these verses again...

*One thing I ask from the LORD,*
*this only do I seek:*
*that I may dwell in the house of the LORD*
*all the days of my life,*
*to gaze on the beauty of the LORD*
*and to seek him in his temple.*
*For in the day of trouble*
*he will keep me safe in his dwelling;*
*he will hide me in the shelter of his sacred tent*
*and set me high upon a rock.*
*Then my head will be exalted*
*above the enemies who surround me;*
*at his sacred tent I will sacrifice with shouts of joy;*
*I will sing and make music to the LORD.*

When we practice this discipline of dwelling in His presence; being still and waiting on Him to fight on our behalf, we develop a confidence in Him that cannot be shaken. In times of trouble, we will be confident that He will keep us safe in His dwelling. This confidence inspires us to bring a sacrifice of praise before Him and our lives become a song and a melody for others to hear; a song that tells of His goodness and faithfulness and glory. It is also a song we sing to ourselves! A song that reminds us to believe and remain confident in the promise that we WILL see goodness in the land of the living! In this season of great pain and sorrow and loneliness and constant change, I can remain confident in this...I will see the goodness of the Lord if I wait on the Lord...if I remain strong and take courage and wait on the Lord! This promise is true for you, too. I have no idea who will pick up this book and read these words, but I am confident that the Lord has called me to write them and I am certain that He desires to use my experience and the words He is giving me to bless YOU! If you are reading this book, these words were poured into my heart for YOU! Your journey may look nothing like mine, but His word is living and active and when it is spoken it never returns void, but it accomplishes His intended purpose.

I hope my story has somehow blessed you. I realize it may be a difficult story to read, but I hope it is a story that speaks of deep abiding joy, hope, comfort, God's goodness and faithfulness, and the victory over trials and suffering that comes when we place our faith and trust in Jesus. James 1:1-4 says "Count it all joy, my brothers, when you meet trials of various kinds, for you know that the testing of your faith produces steadfastness. And let steadfastness have its full effect, that you may be perfect and complete, lacking in nothing." (ESV) I realize how monumentally difficult it is to "count it all joy"! I DO!!! I hope and pray that in no way, shape, form, or fashion the victories and moments of hope and joy I experienced in the midst of my suffering seem as if they came naturally or easily. They DIDN'T!!! At times they did, but for the most part, each victory and moment of celebration and praise was the result of an all-out gut-wrenching, bloody battle to believe and not be overcome by my emotions (which included anger, doubt, confusion, despair, being forsaken, feeling forgotten, dread, and every other painful emotion you can think of), but I also managed to soar on the emotions that brought comfort and peace to my heart. That is the reality of grief. It involves a tangled mess of emotions even for someone with mountain moving faith! But, when we know that the Lord is fighting for us and

*An Unfamiliar Path...*

with us, we have confidence and determination to stay in the battle until the victory comes. That is my prayer for you if you are facing a giant in your life right not...STAY IN THE BATTLE TIL THE VICTORY COMES! When you are too weary to sling the Sword, remember the Lord fights for you; you need only be still (Exodus 14:14)!

## Healed

Healing...takes...time!!! To some degree, we all have different definitions of what healing looks like. Sometimes, healing is accompanied by a complete restoration of functioning. Other times, healing occurs, but full functioning is not restored. Several years ago, I broke my shoulder and had to eventually have a shoulder replacement. My shoulder is healed, but I have limited mobility, loss of strength, and I still often experience aches and pains related to the injury and repair to my normal anatomy. That is kind of how healing has been for me. I believe the Lord has healed my heart and, for the most part, it is functioning well. Nevertheless, there are times when my heart hurts, and the trauma of grief has in some way impaired my capacity to love and dream and celebrate life's joyous events. Maybe more healing will come and restore my heart to an even healthier state, maybe the fullest extent of healing has taken place and my heart will continue to have a "limp" and some scar tissue that limits its functioning. If you are experiencing the pain and anguish of grief, I want to encourage you to seek the One who heals! In order for Him to heal your heart, He must have access. He can't heal what we aren't willing to reveal. Pour out your heart to Him in all honesty...lay it before Him...bloody, bruised...mangled...scared...whatever condition it is in. I promise you He can be trusted, but the healing you desire can only come from Him, the Great Physician. It is scary to bring those deep wounds to Him, I know, but the truth is, it is the only way to have true healing that not only mends but transforms our hearts in the process.

For me, the two things that have brought the most healing to my heart are hope and joy that I have constantly and consistently found

257

as a result of coming into His presence. When I take the time to bring my hurts to Him and rest in His love, I find hope (expectant anticipation) because I am confident that He sees me, loves me, and is working for my good. Abiding in Him (staying connected to Him) not only produces joy, it makes out joy complete (John 15:11). When I rest in Him, Psalm 16:11 comes to life… *"You make known to me the path of life; in your presence there is fullness of joy; at your right hand are pleasures forevermore."* (ESV). In 1 Thessalonians 4:13, we are reminded that as believers, we do not grieve like those who do not know Jesus, we grieve with HOPE. We have hope that we will one day see our loved ones who are in Christ. We have hope that He will redeem our brokenness. We have hope that He will heal our pain and restore our joy. Hope is a powerful force, and it is what has propelled me forward on this journey when I didn't have the strength to move myself due to the heaviness of grief. I recently read the following in an article written by John Piper (sorry it isn't in the bibliography because I cannot locate the original source).

> "There is a paradox in the way God is honored through hope-filled grief. One might think that the only way he could be honored would be to cry less or get over the ache more quickly. But there is another way God is honored in our grieving. When we taste the loss so deeply because we loved so deeply and treasured God's gift — and God in his gift — so passionately that the loss cuts the deeper and the longer, and yet in and through the depths and the lengths of sorrow we never let go of God, and feel him never letting go of us — in that longer sorrow he is also greatly honored, because the length of it reveals the magnitude of our sense of loss for which we do not forsake God. At every moment of the lengthening grief, we turn to him, not away from him. And therefore, the length of it is a way of showing him to be ever-present, enduringly sufficient." His words seemed to echo so much of what God has

been speaking to my heart lately...reminding me of
the need for hope to FILL the empty places carved in
my heart by grief. As my grief lingers and at times
takes over like a tsunami, I cling to HOPE...I cling to
Him and I remember that He clings to me. He is
indeed "ever present and enduringly sufficient."

This is a wonderful description of hope-filled grief! Sadly, people
around us can often grow uncomfortable with our extended seasons of
grief. Some will question if you are "stuck". Others might grow weary of
your tears and anguish and distance themselves from you for one reason
or another. However, when they see and hear HOPE and JOY in the
midst of our pain, they tend to have a better understanding of our grief
and the reality that sorrow and joy can and do coexist in the process of
grieving. They see that, although at times miniscule, we are indeed
"moving forward." There have definitely been moments I have
questioned the duration and intensity of my grief as time has gone by.
Piper's words help bring to life an important reality. When we lose
someone we have loved deeply, we will grieve deeply. Through this deep
grief, God is glorified when we continue to rest in Him with hope and
confidence in His goodness, faithfulness, and love for us. Here is how I
picture the effects of grief on the heart. Some losses are easier to
recover from. The object of our loss (be it a person, dream, job,
whatever) may not have been deeply rooted in the fabric or our heart.
When the loss occurs, only a small void remains and it is easy to fill the
void and overcome the grief by focusing on the many other joys of life.
On the other hand, some losses (loss of a child, spouse, loved one) seem
like a 100 year old oak tree has been ripped from the soil of our heart,
leaving a cavernous, consuming void. Its roots were deeply embedded
throughout every part of our heart. The loss is traumatic, wounding, and
scarring! BUT, when we allow HOPE to FILL the enormous void left
behind, we can trust that in due time, something beautiful will grow.
The soil of HOPE fills the void left by that mighty oak and prepares a
place for God to work and plant and grow. Just like a farmer plants his

259

seed in good soil and trusts that something will grow, when we allow HOPE to fill the void in our heart caused by loss, it is not a matter of IF something good will grow in its place...it is just a matter of WHEN. That is how I picture HOPE-FILLED grief. It is allowing the hope we have in Jesus to FILL the void and allowing God to plant and tend to new dreams and joy and passions and purpose and love that has been lost, and trusting that in due time, something beautiful will grow. Not IF...but WHEN! His timing is perfect and He is faithful to His promise to give us the desires of our heart as we delight in Him. I love that I can ask Him to plant those seeds/desires in my heart (Psalm 37:4). I wouldn't necessarily choose for something new to take the place of what I had with Mike, but the mighty oak tree that he was has been removed, and I am allowing hope to fill the void, and I am waiting patiently (not always though) for whatever God plans to grow in its place. And while I wait, I am learning even more about who He really is, and I am learning to more consistently rest in His love and grace. Psalm 126:5 says "Those who sow in tears will reap with shouts of joy." (HCSB). I have shed many tears on this soil of hope that I am allowing to fill the void, and I am trusting that these tears will be used to water the seeds He is planting and I will continue to reap a harvest of joy in the days and years to come. At times, these were just words I had to believe were true despite what I felt. They were just words to me, hidden and blurred behind the dense fog of grief. As the fog continues to lift, the realty and trustworthiness of these words is becoming more and more vivid and less of an illusion. It takes time!

My primary goal the past five years has been to focus on my kids and to help them navigate and survive the trauma of losing their dad so early in life. I was pretty much in survival mode and in much need of some trauma care. God has been faithful to meet me right where I was and with exactly what I needed. I can honestly say, I wouldn't have made it through a single day had I not consumed every ounce of grace He was willing to pour out. Sadly, I am sure there were days I failed to drink from His fountain of grace and living water, and on those days I wallowed in self-pity and despair was my company rather than the sweet, satisfying, liberating presence of Jesus. Five years down the road and with two amazing kids that have grown into healthy, happy adults, it is time for me to dream again and follow God with excitement and anticipation into whatever it is He has for me in this season of life. It has been such a labor of love and such an important part of my healing journey to gather my journals into this book and share about the many wonderful ways the Lord has blessed and sustained us along the way. Ultimately, my goal is to share our story for His glory. As we have stubbornly and steadfastly believed and stepped out in faith, we have seen God do what only He could do time and time again. He has done exceedingly, abundantly more that we could have ever even thought to ask or could have possibly imagined (Ephesians 3:20-21). Psalm 40:5 sums up the cry of my heart when I reflect back on all we have seen God do for us and in us, *"LORD my God, You have done many things. Your wonderful works and your plans for us; none can compare with You. If I were to report and speak of them, they are more than can be told."* (HCSB). Thank you for joining me on this journey! I pray that you have been blessed and encouraged! I pray that you have seen the glory of Jesus as you have read our story! I pray that you have felt His nearness and tasted of His goodness and been blessed by His grace and love for you.

# *Your Story...*

Take some time to list the wonderful works you have seen the LORD do on your behalf. Ask the Father to give you boldness to tell of His great love and of His Son, Jesus who made a way for us to experience His love and presence for all eternity! I pray that you will continue to tell YOUR STORY!

# ABOUT THE AUTHOR

Lori is a mother, a friend, a teacher, and most importantly a follower of Jesus.  Her passions involve teaching God's word, writing, and encouraging others to deepen their understanding of and faith in God through discipleship, mentoring, and Christian counseling.

Lori's desire for this publication is for God's name to be lifted high, for His true character to be displayed, and for others to read it and catch a glimpse of His amazing grace and indescribable love in action. She and her husband, Mike, originally published *An Unfamiliar Path* as a means to generate funds to support a 501c3 ministry Mike developed. The name of the ministry was Isaiah 42:16 Ministry. The ministry was created in an effort to come alongside others who are traveling unfamiliar paths while dealing with chronic, terminal, or debilitating medical issues.  Through the Isaiah 42:16 Ministry, they were able to raise and distribute over $10,000 to families in need.  Although the ministry was dissolved after Mike passed away, Lori continues to walk alongside others facing similar circumstances and has a heart to walk alongside other widows as they navigate the turbulent waters of grief and widowhood. The proceeds from the sale of this book continue to be used to bless others.

Lori enjoys opportunities to speak at churches and other groups. If you are interested in contacting her about an opportunity to share her story and encourage others, she can be reached by email at loriuhearn@gmail.com

*"I will lead the blind by ways they have not known, along unfamiliar paths I will guide them; I will turn the darkness into light before them and make the rough places smooth. These are the things I will do; I will not forsake them."*
### Isaiah 42:16

# Bibliography

1.Chambers, Oswald. *My Utmost for His Highest*. Uhrichsville, OH: Barbour Pub., 2007. Print.

2.Camp, Jeremy. "Walk by Faith." *Jeremy Camp Live*. BEC Recordings, 2009. CD.

3.Nockels, Christy. "Grace Flows down." *OneDay Live*. Sparrow Label Group, 2006. CD.

4.Jobe, Kari. "How He Loves." *Prepare the Way*. Integrity Music, 2010. CD

5.Carmichael, Amy, and David Hazard. *I Come Quietly to Meet You: an Intimate Journey in God's Presence*. Minneapolis, MN: Bethany House, 2005. Print.

6.Redman, Matt. "Blessed be Your Name." *Where Angels Fear to Tread*. Survivor Records, 2002. CD.

7.Cowman, Charles E. *Streams in the Desert*. Grand Rapids, MI: Zondervan, 1996. Print.

8.Young, Sarah. *Jesus Calling*. [S.l.]: Integrity, 2007. Print.

9.Tomlin, Chris. "Strength Will Rise." *America's 25 Best Praise & Worship Songs*. Integrity Music/Word, 1997. CD.

10.Hall, Charlie. "On Christ the Solid Rock." *Passion: Hymns Ancient and Modern.* EMI Christian Music Group, 2004. CD

11.Tomlin, Chris. "Glory in the Highest." *Christmas Songs.* Sparrow Records, 2009. CD

12.Camp, Jeremy. "Empty Me." *Jeremy Camp Live.* BEC Recordings, 2009. CD.

13.Redman, Matt. "You Never Let Go." *Passion: Everything Glorious.* Sparrow Records, 2006. CD.

14.Nordeman, Nicole. "How Deep the Father's Love For Us." *Nicole Nordeman: The Ultimate Collection.* Sparrow Records, 2006. CD

15.Baloche, Paul. "How Great Thou Art." *Our God Saves.* Integrity Music, 2007. CD.

16.Story, Laura. "Blessings." *Blessings.* INO Records, 2011. CD

17.Millard, Bart. "Keep Singing." *Undone.* INO Records, 2004. CD.

18.Hurnard, Hannah. *Hinds' Feet on High Places.* Wheaton, IL: Living, 1986. Print.

19.Hall, Mark. "Tis So Sweet to Trust in Jesus." *The Altar and the Door.* Reunion Records, 2007. CD.

20.Jensen, Tammy. "Jesus I am Resting, Resting." *Resting.* Tammy Jensen, 2007. CD.

21.Maher, Matt. "You Were on the Cross." *Alive Again.* Essential Records, 2011. CD.

Made in the USA
Lexington, KY
24 June 2019